RESPONSIBLE CONDUCT

RESPONSIBLE CONDUCT

Principles of Christian Ethics

J. DOUMA

Translated by Nelson D. Kloosterman

P.O. BOX 817 • PHILLIPSBURG • NEW JERSEY 08865-0817

Previously published in Dutch as the tenth fully revised edition of *Verantwoord handelen. Inleiding in de christelijke ethiek,* by Kok Voorhoeve, Kampen, 1997. The first and second editions appeared as volume 7 of the series Ethisch Commentaar (Amsterdam, 1975). The third through the ninth editions appeared as volume 1 of the series Ethische Bezinning (Kampen, 1983–95).

Italics within Scripture quotations indicate emphasis added.

Page design by Tobias Design
Typesetting by Michelle Feaster

Printed in the United States of America

Library of Congress Cataloging-in-Publication Data

Douma, Jochem, 1931–
[Verantwoord handelen. English]
Responsible conduct : principles of Christian ethics / J. Douma ; translated by Nelson D. Kloosterman.
p. cm.
Includes bibliographical references (p.) and index.
ISBN 0-87552-572-5 (pbk.)
1. Christian ethics. I. Title.

BJ1251.D6813 2003
241—dc21

2002045041

Contents

Preface to the Tenth Dutch Edition

I am glad that interest continues to be shown in this "Introduction to Christian Ethics." Because the third edition has not been revised since its publication in 1983, and since that edition has a number of shortcomings, the time has come for a revision. This, then, is the tenth edition in new clothes. It is my heartfelt hope that this edition will also serve the needs of both individuals and educational institutions.

My thanks to readers who have pointed out defects in earlier editions and who with their questions have motivated me to rewrite several portions of the book.

Hardenberg, June 1997

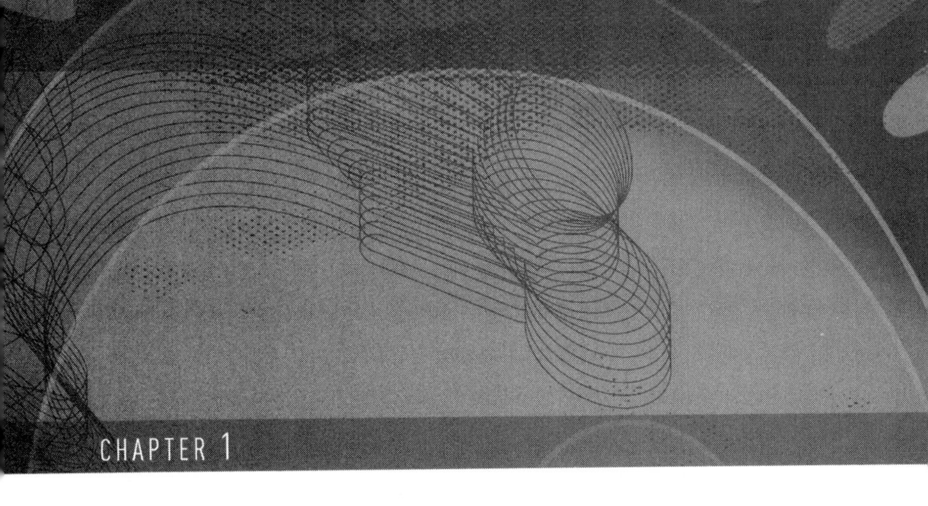

CHAPTER 1

Morality and Ethics

EVERYBODY DEALS WITH THEM

Anyone who reads the daily newspaper is told about what is happening at home and abroad. We read about governments brought down, about war and poverty in the world, about airplane and train accidents. Scandals of various kinds are daily news. Alongside the major news, there are also the minor reports about births, weddings, and deaths. Books are reviewed, merchandise is advertised, and wonderful vacations are offered.

So we take in a mountain of information. But that is not the end of the matter. We also form *judgments* about various matters. The newspaper helps with that, not only by reporting facts, but also by providing background information. Why is a certain government being brought down? Has it been oppressing its citizens and violating their rights? What lies behind the crimes of drug users and child killers? If there has been a railway accident, was the engineer perhaps negligent?

We form judgments, even about those minor matters. We cannot purchase everything offered to us. Often we don't even want to, because we object to what is being offered. A vacation package surpassing our financial capabilities we reject as irresponsible. Even an obituary can evoke a judgment from us. We remember the deceased person whom we once knew as either a good or a bad person.

Let me list a number of expressions used in the preceding paragraphs: *oppress, violate rights, responsible, negligent, good,* and *bad.*

These terms make it obvious that every day we deal with morality and ethics, whether or not we are even aware of it. In morality and ethics, we focus on human acts of commission and omission, and we offer our judgment about them. Inevitably in that connection, we use words like *good* and *bad,* depending on whether we want to indicate our approval or disapproval.

TERMINOLOGY

I just used two words: *morality* and *ethics*. What is the difference between them? These are words with a foreign ancestry, coming from Greek and Latin. *Ethics* comes from the Greek words *ethos* and *ēthos*. It appears in the New Testament. We read that Jesus went to the Mount of Olives, as was His custom or habit (Greek: *kata to ethos,* Luke 22:39). The writer of the book of Acts mentions that the Romans did not have the custom or habit (*ethos*) of handing a defendant over without granting him an opportunity to face his accuser (Acts 25:16). In addition to "custom" or "habit," the word *ethos* can also refer to the English plural, "mores." In Philippi, people accused Paul and Silas of teaching mores (*ethē*) that were not lawful for Romans to receive or observe (Acts 16:21). In one of his letters, Paul quotes the proverb of the pagan poet Menander: "Evil company corrupts good habits [*ēthē*]" (1 Cor. 15:33).

In some manuals of ethics, a distinction is made between *ethos* as morality in the sense of custom and habit, and *ēthos* as morality in the sense of character and disposition. However, that distinction is rarely visible. We might rather say that both senses merge. Disposition comes to expression in custom, while custom presupposes a particular disposition.

It is surely interesting to know that *ethos* and *ēthos* can refer to a habitat (of people or animals). That sheds light on the deep significance that habit and custom have in human life. Custom is no merely external matter. We habit-ate in our customs; our customs constitute the milieu in which we exist. From a person's moral behavior, we can figure out where he is at home.

Enough, then, about the word *ethics*. Where does the word *morality* come from? From the Latin word *mos*, which is related to *metiri*, "to measure." We may be brief at this point, since the Latin word *mos* has the same meaning as the Greek words *ethos* and *ēthos*.

Our exploration of the meaning of the Greek and Latin words thus yields no difference between them. But we may still distinguish between the English words *ethics* and *morality*. Not everybody does so. Here is a somewhat outdated illustration of that: a Protestant theologian specializing in ethics is often called an "ethicist," while his Roman Catholic colleague is called a "moral theologian."

Personally, I distinguish between ethics and morality this way: *morality* consists of the entirety of traditional and dominant customs, while *ethics* is reflection upon those customs. I can describe morality as it existed among Greeks, Romans, and medieval Christians, and as it exists today in various expressions. But when I describe morality, I don't need to furnish a judgment. I offer a judgment in *ethics*. So ethics is reflection upon morality (or morals). People do this or that (morality), but are they right in so doing (ethics)? Clearly, ethics cannot exist without morality, although morality need not involve ethics. One cannot make a judgment about whether an act is good or bad if he has no knowledge of that act. But one can certainly describe an act or an entire morality without at the same rendering a judgment regarding that description.

The difference between morality and ethics can also be expressed this way: we could produce an individual ethics, but we could never sustain an individual morality. An individual man or woman could write a manual of ethics. But morality is always group morality. Morality is a social phenomenon, something ethics does not need to be.

Other terms are used for what we refer to as *ethics* and *morality*. We too could use other terms than *morality* and *ethics*. People speak of "mores" (in the sense of morality) and of "moral teaching" (in the sense of ethics). Mores are the rules of conduct of a community, while moral teaching is reflection upon those rules of conduct.

The terms *morality* and *ethics* have become so familiar and so useful internationally that we prefer them to those other terms. Moreover, nowadays we use terms like *mores* or *conventions* more in the sense of group conventions or popular conventions: conventional times for eating, conventional dishes, customs of politeness, of social gatherings, etc. To such phenomena we pay little attention when we speak about morality. Equally little attention is paid to *etiquette*, although it might appear that etiquette involves ethics. Dutch ethicist J. de Graaf (1969, 52) has called etiquette "a miniature ethics," but that is misleading, since the word *etiquette* comes from French, not Greek, deriving from an old verb, *estiquer* (to fix), which had the meaning of "etiquette" (politeness) only after 1600.

If we gather together a number of things, we can clarify what ethics does and does not involve. There are personal *habits* (carrying our keys in the left pocket or right pocket, napping at noontime, and the like). There are cultural habits or *conventions* (times and ways of eating, celebrations of milestones, forms of interpersonal interaction, and the like). There is *morality* (customs in which the contrast between good and bad occupies our attention). There is *ethics* (reflection upon morality). The first two, important as they may be for everyday life, fall beyond the scope of this book. Here we are paying attention to morality and ethics.

RELEVANCE

Ethics as reflection upon morality has always existed, even though it might not have been described this way. In the Old Testament, there is no particular word for "habit," but habits are still present. When Jacob's daughter, Dinah, was violated, her brothers were grieved and very angry about the disgraceful thing done in Israel, "a thing which ought not to be done" (Gen. 34:7). Tamar said precisely the same thing to her half-brother, Amnon, who was intending to disgrace her (2 Sam. 13:12).

In contrast to folly, there is wisdom, *chokma*, which was to be taught to the youth, so they would choose good and reject evil. Here we think especially of the book of Proverbs, designed to instill cleverness in the ignorant and to endow youth with knowledge and circumspection (Prov. 1:4). Some have called *moesar* the Hebrew word for ethics, which in Greek is translated *paideia* and in English *discipline.* All good nurture embodies a lot of ethics! Nevertheless, interest in ethics varies significantly from one era to another. Why is interest in ethics so great today, compared with fifty years ago? The answer is simple. Morals contain the element of continuity and fixity. They bear an impersonal, social, and strongly obvious character. Within a society that changes very little, ethical instruction will not encounter significant problems. But today we observe that traditional morality has been cast into doubt, or rejected, at almost every point. This is very obvious in the area of sexual morality, which has undergone a comprehensive revolution. Modern man views himself as mature, and is not restrained by comments like "People don't do that." Tradition holds no sway any longer, nothing once thought to be self-evident is viewed that way any longer, and the personal, rather than the social, motif must now be considered decisive.

So the term *morals* seems outdated. Or do new morals come into existence? Does everybody really do what is right in his or her own eyes, or does our environment determine our conduct more than we sometimes imagine? The answer to the question concerning good and evil is apparently not just a personal matter, but also a social matter.

We must consider one other factor. Earlier people lived mostly in their closed little worlds: the world of their family, their village, their city, and their country. Attention has always been paid to distant events, but people learned of them without being affected by them. Nowadays we are growing into one world, where all people are gradually becoming our neighbors. Television has contributed significantly to this development. At the same time, we are coming to see that we are dealing with the same moral problems as everybody else in the world. Take, for example, environmental issues. Consider the contrast, in terms of wealth and poverty, between North and South, or West and East. Think of nuclear weapons, which can impact the whole world with their destructive power. All these issues are discussed in ethics.

SUBDIVISIONS WITHIN ETHICS

If we wish to delve more deeply into the subject of ethics, we can do that in various ways. For example, we can divide ethics into (1) descriptive ethics, (2) normative ethics, (3) special ethics, and (4) metaethics. Let's look at the particular contours of these subdisciplines.

Descriptive ethics provides a description of habits and morals appearing in various cultures past and present. Especially cultural anthropologists and sociologists concern themselves with this discipline. If ethics consists of reflection upon morality, as I proposed earlier, then such reflection is always evaluative. But that does not apply to describing morals, which is interested only in reporting and not evaluating. Therefore, strictly speaking, the phrase "descriptive *ethics*" is incorrect; this discipline involves mere description of morality, not of ethics. No matter, the phrase has become familiar terminology, and everybody admits that ethics contains a description of morality as one of its elements. If you want to reflect upon morality (which is ethics), you need to know what you are talking about (namely, morality). To help with that, descriptive studies can be quite useful.

In *normative ethics*, we proceed from a norm, a standard or measure that indicates how we should live. So here we are not describing what morality is, but declaring what it should be. You can describe the moral aspects of slavery, polygamy, euthanasia, and violence in sports (as in, "This is how people view these things"), but you can also evaluate these moral aspects according to a particular norm (as in, "This is how one should view these things"). In this book, I will be dealing almost exclusively with normative ethics, proceeding from the norm of God's word as we find it in Holy Scripture.

Special ethics is a specialization within normative ethics. Today nobody can keep up with the entire field of ethics. One person specializes in medical ethics, another in environmental ethics, a third in business ethics, a fourth in sexual ethics, and so forth. We can study the professional ethics of social workers, nurses, lawyers, and journalists, and study the code of ethics established for each profession. Each of these is a subdivision of normative ethics.

METAETHICS

We need to spend a bit more time with *metaethics*. This is the term given to that section of ethics that was once called philosophical or critical or formal ethics. Frequently this section was included with normative ethics. That is no surprise, since this subdivision deals with the fundamental questions of ethics. What is the meaning of words like *good, evil, duty*, and *norm?* Is our action free or determined? Is moral conduct relative, so that what is good in a certain place at a certain time is evil in another place and time? An example frequently mentioned is that of an eighteenth-century missionary who was speaking with an Eskimo girl about love toward God and neighbor. That girl thought she had shown love toward her neighbor when she brought an aged, sick woman, who was unable to die, out to a steep precipice, at the woman's request, in order to push her off. What one person would call murder or punishable assisted suicide, the other calls a form of loving one's neighbor!

Metaethics has received widespread attention within analytic linguistic philosophy. One important matter is the character of an ethical assertion. To analyze this, the ethical assertion is placed alongside other kinds of assertions.

Assertions can appear to be grammatically identical, while nevertheless being of differing kinds. Consider the following assertions:

1. The moon is a heavenly body.
2. The moon is pretty.
3. The moon is a useful object for mankind.

The first assertion contains a fact that can be verified. The second assertion provides a personal evaluation involving my feelings. I find the moon pretty. It would have been strange had I said, "I find the moon to be a heavenly body." The third assertion offers a value judgment: I find it good that the moon is used by mankind, for example, by building a space laboratory on the moon.

The first and second statements are not ethical assertions, unlike the third, which contains a number of ethical aspects. Is it indeed true that the moon is a useful object for mankind?

Would it not be far better for the environment and for other things, if mankind did not use the moon any longer? One person says that it is (morally) good that mankind develop his use of the moon; another says that such a thing is wrong. In metaethics we penetrate further. Why do we call something good or wrong? Is that simply because an individual or a group finds something good or wrong? Is not moral good or moral evil more than a kind of feeling—in contrast to the view of a certain metaethical position known as emotivism? According to emotivism, an ethical assertion resembles our second assertion above. Just as we find the moon pretty, because we can take a romantic walk in the moonlight, so too moral good and evil depend on our taste. Or are good and evil something all of us must acknowledge because they are just as verifiable as the fact expressed in our first assertion, namely, that the moon is a heavenly body? Is the good measurable, so that it can be translated into terms that everybody can verify? Utilitarians, for example, adopt this view, because they argue that whatever is good fits this principle of measurability: "Good is that which brings the greatest happiness to the greatest number of people."

No matter how stimulating this subdivision of ethics may be, we will not be discussing it in this book. To be sure, metaethics always plays a role in the background of normative ethics, as we shall see in what follows. Metaethics is just as value-laden as normative ethics. It is more than an exercise in tidy ethical thinking, where we reflect on precisely what we mean by such words as *good, evil, virtue, vice, norm,* and *duty.*

J. de Graaf describes metaethics as that branch of ethical science "which, as it were, looks over the shoulder of the practitioner of normative ethics and special ethics, and proposes a theory concerning the possibility or impossibility of verifying ethical-normative assertions" (1986, 3). But looking over someone's shoulder and then proposing a theory can occur in very different ways. People can develop theories that reduce ethical judgments to assertions of feeling. Or theories can be developed which point to the meaningful connection between ethical judgments and the unfolding of life in terms of the commands that God has given for that unfolding. But we will return to this later. First we need a bit more insight into what ethics involves.

Literature

De Graaf, J. 1969. *De ethiek van het immoralisme.* 3d ed. Nijkerk: G. F. Callenbach.

De Graaf, J. 1986. *Elementair begrip van de ethiek.* 4th ed. Utrecht: Bohn Scheltema Holkema.

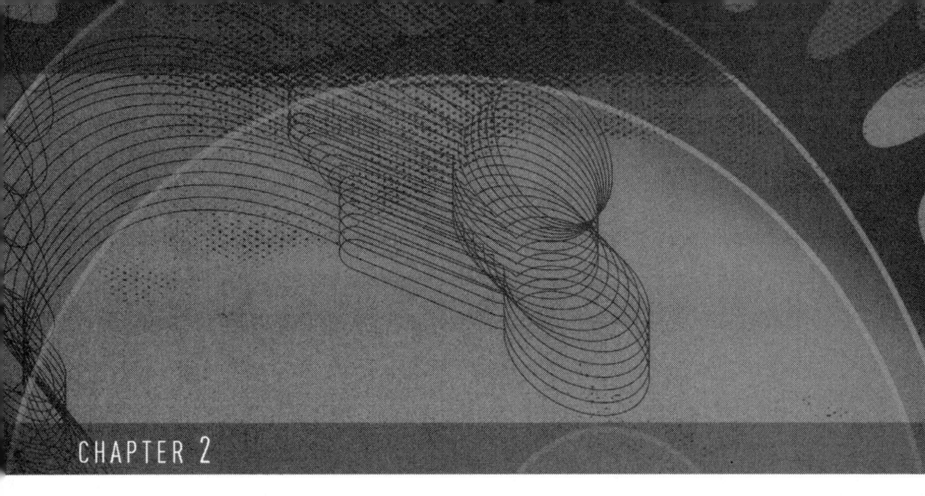

The Definition of Christian Ethics

THE PURPOSE OF THIS CHAPTER

In the first chapter, I delineated what is covered in ethics. Terms like *good, evil, norm, duty*, and *virtue* play a role here. But we need to delimit our subject a bit more precisely. We can do that best by means of a definition. The word *definition* literally means a "limitation" or "specification." By means of those "specs" or limits, we identify the area within which ethics works. We also want to add something to the word *ethics* at this point. This book is dealing, after all, with *Christian* ethics.

So we use a definition to identify the boundaries. In so doing, we also indicate what is not covered in ethics. Well then, what lies within and what lies outside of ethics? The definition I use goes like this:

> *Christian ethics is reflection upon moral conduct in light of the perspective offered us in Holy Scripture.*

The first part of this definition we saw already in chapter 1: ethics is reflection upon moral conduct. But I need to say some more about that, in order to indicate more precisely what properly belongs to ethical reflection. At least seven characteristics interest us in this connection.

HUMAN CONDUCT

Moral conduct is *human* conduct. The behavior of plants and animals lies beyond the scope of Christian ethics. True, we do speak of the loyalty of a dog, the industry of ants, and the laziness of pigs. Loyalty, industry, and laziness have something to do with ethics. But when we speak of these things in connection with animals, we are speaking figuratively. Animals act on the basis of instinct or training, and we don't describe their behavior as having a moral quality.

This observation, though it seems self-evident, does already embody a choice. In environmental ethics, some draw the boundaries of the moral community to include much more than just people. In opposition to anthropocentric thinking (i.e., thinking in which mankind is central), some people include within the moral community mammals or all animals capable of feeling pain. When I don't draw the boundaries that widely, you should not conclude from this that we have no place in our morality or ethics to consider animals. Moral human conduct also involves things like plants and animals. Anyone mistreating animals or polluting the environment is acting morally wrongly. But making that assertion does not require us to include animals as members of the moral community. Animals act instinctively and are unable to make choices. Ethics is interested in reflecting on behavior for which we are responsible. We do not ascribe such responsibility to any animal. We certainly do have a responsibility toward animals, but animals don't have a responsibility toward us. An animal cannot act immorally toward a person, though a person can act wrongly toward an animal.

NORMATIVE CONDUCT

Moral conduct is also *normative* conduct. Not every human act possesses a normative character. People also act by instinct or under compulsion, doing things they can hardly resist (yawning, dream-induced acts, sleepwalking, satisfying hunger and thirst, and the like). These actions all have a "must" character. This English word indicates that we cannot act otherwise. However, morality deals with actions that have an "ought" character, that is, with things that *should* be thus and so. There is a difference between appropriate and inappropriate conduct. And the reason we find one act appropriate and another inappropriate is that acts are measured according to a particular, valid norm. The word *norm* comes from the Latin and means "measure" or "standard." So we are dealing with actions flowing from choices for which a person can be held responsible. That explains the title of this book!

That we are responsible stands out more clearly when we think for a moment about people we *cannot* hold responsible. Think of small infants and the mentally disturbed. They lack, either partially or completely, any capacity to choose. When they do strange things, we smooth it over by saying, "He's only a baby," or "This patient can't help it." In this way, we are observing that they are not yet or no longer in a position to act morally. Indeed, we can speak about a compulsive or instinctive "must," but "ought" presupposes freedom and a sense of responsibility.

Without freedom, morality is unimaginable. Few people think alike about the measure of freedom that a person possesses for acting, whether in personal or collective relationships. The two extreme opinions are *determinism* and *indeterminism*. Determinism says that every human action is fixed. Human action is not free, but entirely conditioned, fixed by cause and effect. We can go in only one direction. Indeterminism says that we can go in many directions. We act in freedom, and although we do one particular thing, we could have done other things.

Both viewpoints are extreme, and therefore unreal. Limitation and freedom go together. People are strongly conditioned biologically, historically, socially, and culturally. In a biography, for example, we can relate someone's behavior to the family from which he came, the time in which he lived (we even say, "He was a child of his time"), the social group to which he belonged, or even the climate of cultural opinion in which he was reared. On the other hand, people actually do develop their own behavioral style. With J. de Graaf, we can say that the context of historical, social, and cultural circumstances, and of a particular psychological orientation and disposition, "determines [conduct] not in the manner of a one-sided prescription that would arise from this context, but it does condition a person; it circumscribes the area within which the choice among kinds of behavior will be able to be made. . . . So one cannot choose among all imaginable possibilities (indeterminism), but only among a number of real and attainable alternatives" (1986, 22). That strikes me as a balanced view of the room that most people have to maneuver as they ask themselves self-consciously why they would do one thing and not another. They are not acting instinctively, like an animal, nor is their acting entirely determined, but they possess freedom to choose, a choice made in terms of various norms.

IN TERMS OF THE ASPECT OF GOOD AND EVIL

Morality is normative conduct, but of a certain kind. It is conduct viewed in terms of the aspect of *good and evil.* Our definition says that ethics deals with *moral* conduct. Not every normative action is moral action. Let me illustrate this in a number of ways.

If you want to pass an exam, you need to master the assigned material, so that you can give answers that are right and not wrong. What is normative for an exam is whether the answers are *right or wrong,* in the sense of correct or incorrect. If you give incorrect answers on an exam, then you fall short intellectually. But we wouldn't say that you thereby acted immorally. A mistake or blunder is not a lie.

If you build a house, you need to build according to technical norms, so that you do not end up with a monstrosity. We evaluate a professional builder in terms of *good and bad.* But a bad builder need not be a bad man in the moral sense of that word.

We measure the acumen of a businessman in terms of his economic insights. He needs to know what is *efficient and inefficient* for his business. If a businessman sells his products far below cost, out of sympathy for poor people, that may evoke moral respect, while at the same time being economically irresponsible.

An artist's painting we evaluate in terms of whether it is

tasteful or ugly. Some morally reputable people fail as artists, and some great artists are not too fussy when it comes to morals.

A judge's pronouncements we evaluate as *lawful or unlawful.* Should he render a verdict in conflict with prevailing laws, his unlawful verdict might still rest on good moral grounds, in which case the prevailing laws give expression to a bad morality.

In all the illustrations I have given, human actions can be measured in terms of norms that people can transgress. But these transgressions are not necessarily *moral* transgressions.

PROPERLY MOTIVATED CONDUCT

Now that I have clarified the definition of ethics somewhat, I want to supplement these three aspects of ethics with a number of others. If we are dealing with human *conduct,* we are looking at more than the exterior of that conduct. Naturally, we must pay attention to the exterior, to the *act* belonging to conduct. Good intentions are not enough; we must translate them into action. Obviously, ethics is concerned with that action. But at this point I wish to emphasize the interior aspect of human conduct. Moral conduct must also be *properly motivated* conduct.

In our ethical reflection, we must avoid taking too much hay on our fork, and so ethics does not reflect upon every action that might be called normative. But we must also avoid drawing the boundary too narrowly, which would happen if we looked at moral conduct without inquiring about what lies *behind* that conduct. What is my motivation; what drives me to do this and not that?

Especially the great philosopher Immanuel Kant pointed to the "disposition" of a person as something essential to morality. Legalism means that we do something because the law commands it. It must be done, but we don't do it from the heart. We fill out our tax returns honestly, but only because we must; we do it out of well-considered self-interest. Suppose we were audited and got into trouble! Now, if we act that way, we may well be acting legally, but we're not acting morally. We are not acting from the heart. We are not acting out of genuine "respect for the law." Then our *will* is not good, says Kant. For him, the only good is a good will.

The element of motive is essential for ethics. This is obvious as soon as we intuitively sense the difference between the objective action and the subjective attitude of the person acting. Recall the Pharisee in the Bible who, looking down his nose at the beggar, prayed fervently and fasted publicly—but he was doing all this to be seen and respected by others. Two people could be doing the same thing, objectively speaking, but we might evaluate their actions completely differently.

EMOTION-LADEN CONDUCT

In our conduct, we are understandably concerned to distinguish between good and evil. Our will is involved when we consider motive. But we may also require that a good moral action possess an *emotional interest* in the person(s) toward whom it is directed. What Kant wrote about disposition is very important. But he was very insistent on eliminating from disposition everything having to do with emotions and passions. Kant's ethics show a strongly cognitive tendency. His view boils down to knowledge and rational motive. But the good moral act is unimaginable apart from the emotional involvement of the person who acts. One who acts strictly on the basis of rules and technique, apart from feelings that are appropriate to those requirements, is morally deficient. Consider the need to put oneself inside the feelings and suffering of another person, and to establish a bond with someone needing our help. Good care is also emotion-laden care.

Emotions of rage, hatred, or even excessive love can so dominate us that we lose sight of responsible action. Correction at this point need not consist of suppressing our emotions. We have received not only understanding and volition, but also emotions. And we need not be ashamed when emotions are expressed in our actions!

VIRTUOUS CONDUCT

In ethics, we also deal with what we call *virtue*. Virtue focuses on the *continuity* of human conduct, whereas motivation focuses on the *depth* of such conduct. When we look at virtue, we inquire about the fact that what makes a person moral is more than a single action. Suppose someone performs an honest deed; we do not then declare that he is an honest person. We cannot determine who a person *is* simply from what he *does*. We saw this already when we discussed motivation, but here that same feature is underscored. In order to move from kind of action to kind of person, we need to see continuity in a particular action. Only when someone's actions are repeatedly honest, fair, or compassionate do we declare that such a person *is* honest, fair, or compassionate. To speak about virtue is to speak about human *character*.

Everybody realizes this. If there were no continuity in

conduct, then we would not be able to trust anybody. We can trust a person because we expect a certain level or kind of (good) action from him. Even when we say, "I don't care for that person," we are proceeding on the basis of a certain kind of expectation. For example, we expect that he or she has an honest character, but we catch him or her in a lie. At that point, we don't say that such a person is a liar. One or two lies don't make one a liar. Similarly, speaking a truth doesn't make someone an honest person. Someone might speak the truth twenty times, but we might yet say, "I still don't trust him!"

Clearly, this aspect has a lot to do with nurture and training. You can train yourself in virtuous conduct. We teach our children to be honest, helpful, sharing, etc. Long ago Aristotle talked about this element of training. Someone who plucks at a harp is not yet a harp*ist*. A harpist is someone who is "good" at playing the harp. Similarly, a person needs to practice and exercise virtue in order to be a "good" or virtuous person. Aristotle even says that only then is a person truly human (see Aristotle [1976] 1986, 91–110).

The question What must we do? asked not only by Aristotle, but also frequently throughout two thousand years of church history, became the question Who must we be? We sense the power of this question especially when people are viewed as examples for others. Anyone who is impressed by another person as an example desires to *be* like his model, rather than simply to *act* like his model.

Nowadays people often talk negatively about virtuosity and virtues. Certain virtues like chastity, obedience, courage, or patriotism are supposedly outdated and should make room for authenticity, professionalism, and plausibility (de Graaf 1972, 9). But this change is only relative. When our own country competes in international sports, loyalty to our nation is perhaps stronger than that of chivalrous medieval knights to their kin and country. Virtues are also subject to changes in emphasis and popularity. What is "in" today may be "out" tomorrow. But the notion of virtue remains.

PURPOSEFUL CONDUCT

We are not yet finished, for another important aspect of conduct is that it is purposeful. We are always interested in answering the question Why are we doing this? (in the sense of For what purpose are we doing this?). This question, in fact, brings us to the outer limit of morality. For our moral conduct often serves purposes which themselves are not of a moral nature. In ethical reflection, this kind of goal is frequently termed a "value" or a "good," although this latter term has become a bit old-fashioned. We could mention quite a number of values, like health, beauty, freedom of expression, religious freedom, democracy, happiness, attaining one's ideals, and serving God. Each one can be described as nonmoral, or, still better, as supramoral. Moreover, we strive to realize such values, not only by moral conduct, but in other ways as well. Take, for example, the value of happiness. If each person behaved well morally, that would certainly advance personal and social happiness. But the happiness of many people is also advanced by, for example, developing their intellectual or aesthetic gifts, or cultivating their business acumen.

We cannot understand morality completely without looking at this question of purpose or goal. Norms and virtues are affected by one another. If we should be doing something, a reason why that thing needs doing should be able to be given.

When we talk about virtues, it is obvious that these are "good" for something. The surgeon's tools look quite different from the farmer's implements, because they are used for a different purpose. Similarly, norms and virtues can differ radically, depending on the values being pursued by an individual or a society.

Values can be subordinated to still other values. Everyone values health, but health can be subordinated to a higher value. A Christian will subordinate health, well-being, or happiness to a higher purpose, namely, serving and honoring God.

We can say that purposeful conduct has much to do with motivation. The question Why are we doing this? deals with motivation as well as purpose. The difference is that with motivation, we are still moving within the moral arena. But when it comes to the purpose of our conduct, we move beyond the moral arena by asking, Why are we doing *this* (as opposed to something else)?

UTILITARIAN OR DEONTOLOGICAL ETHICS?

From the foregoing, it has become clear that an ethical act has various facets. We must look not only at the deed itself, but also at the motivation behind the deed. We must consider the deed (Matt. 7:21–27). Formerly, ethics paid far more attention to this than it does currently. When you read the Old Testament legislation, you will notice that much of it deals with penalties for particular actions. Transgressors are sentenced because they have committed a forbidden deed. Sins committed intentionally, "with a high hand," are differentiated from sins committed unintentionally (Num. 15:22–31; 35:9–28). Someone who accidentally killed his neighbor could flee to one of six cities of refuge in Israel to escape the revenge of the victim's family. Nevertheless, the deed itself was so serious that sometimes the fugitive had to remain in the city of refuge for a long time. If he went outside the boundary of the city, he could become a victim of revenge. The deed of killing, therefore, could not simply be ignored. Bloodshed requires atonement, just as robbery requires restitution.

This provides us with a lesson for today as well. Even when we are not morally liable, we cannot simply ignore our actions that cause someone harm.

Nevertheless, to analyze conduct properly, we cannot limit ourselves to the deed. To evaluate an ethical action properly, we must also look at disposition, as we saw above. "And whatever you do," writes Paul, "do it heartily, as to the Lord and not to men" (Col. 3:23). But one can place too much emphasis on disposition. We do that when we ignore the *consequences* of our actions. True, the deed itself is not the only consideration—nor is the motive. But an isolated emphasis on disposition leaves us with an attitudinal ethics. The German poet Theodor Storm captured the heart of this moral system in four lines:

> The one asks, "What comes after?"
> The other asks only, "Is it right?"
> And this is the difference
> Between freeman and slave.

Apparently this poet considered it slavish to look only at consequences, so that for him, the only proper ethics was an ethics of disposition. The philosopher Kant constructed this kind of ethics. According to Kant, to act on the basis of consequences is to act wrongly. It comes down to having a good will and to doing our duty. A merchant must deal honestly with his customers, not because he would otherwise lose them, but because it is his duty to be honest, even if by being honest he would lose customers.

Now Kant is saying something true here, but still he has become one-sided. If we look again at the verse of Theodor Storm, we can heartily agree that in answering the question of the "slave," we can evaluate the consequences of an action egoistically, merely in terms of ourselves. But we could also be so concerned about our neighbor's well-being that we will not perform an action on account of its consequences, no matter how good the motive for such an action might be. If the "freeman" ignores consequences, he is employing an abstract kind of freedom. We cannot separate our freedom from the consequences of our conduct. Action evokes reaction, and we can be responsible for that reaction as well.

A useful illustration of this is the issue of unilateral disarmament. If a country would get rid of all its weapons because war is always terrible, that might seem to be morally good. Pacifism proceeds from a good disposition. But if the consequence of our pacifism is that other countries have free play to trample over us with threats of blackmail, are we then not responsible for that consequence? A good disposition is not very good at all if it lacks wisdom. And counting the cost is part of wisdom. A king who wants to fight another king must first consider whether with ten thousand soldiers he can defeat his opponent who has twenty thousand soldiers. If he cannot, then he must try to seek conditions of peace (Luke 14:31–32). Such a king may have every right to wage war against his enemy. However, his ethical conduct not only must proceed from a good disposition, but also should consider possible consequences.

There is a Latin proverb that goes like this: *Fiat justitia, pereat mundus,* which means, "Let justice take its course, even if the world should perish." That sounds principled, but it is an unacceptable rule of behavior. If the consequences of my well-intentioned act can be foreseen or avoided, then I am responsible for those consequences. My conduct must indeed proceed from a good disposition, but it must also hit the right target.

Disposition, deed, and consequence are three essential considerations. We may distinguish them, but never separate them.

Thus, we need to avoid imbalance, especially when others confront us with choices. What I have just explained has to do with a dilemma that is easily forced upon us. Supposedly we need to choose between a *utilitarian* and a *deontological* ethics. Utilitarianism focuses on the consequences of an action by inquiring about its benefit. Such benefit need not be egoistical. The British philosophers Jeremy Bentham (1748–1832) and John Stuart Mill (1806–73) defended a utilitarianism that was socially directed. They were interested in *the greatest happiness of the greatest number of people.* If I perform a deed to my personal advantage, but to my neighbor's disadvantage, then it seems evident that I do not desire the greatest happiness for the greatest number of people. The utilitarian wants us to strike a balance when we act. What are the good and the bad consequences of my action? Weigh them against each other, and perform that action which as much as possible maximizes benefit and minimizes harm.

The *deontologist* works in a different way. The Greek word *deon* means "that which ought to happen." We might say that for a deontologist, duty is the focus. He looks not at the consequence of an action, but at normative principles and the disposition, both of which provide direction for deciding what is good and evil. If the norm requires speaking the truth at all times, then we may not lie, even if that might benefit ourselves or others. Law is law and a rule is a rule!

Do we need to choose between these two approaches? Let us consider first the deontological approach. It happens occasionally that we should decide to perform certain actions because God asks us to do them, even though we might injure ourselves. At that point, we are deontologists. We conclude that we must obey God's commandment, even though it *appears* that the consequences of our obedience will be injurious to ourselves. I emphasize that it *appears* that way. For if you believe that God leads your life, you will also believe that what He asks of you is best for you. If a difficult decision is made that does not maximize benefit immediately, then its benefit will appear later. Our horizon for determining benefit extends beyond the grave. Jesus even says that whoever gives up house or brothers or sisters or mother or father or children or fields for His sake and that of the gospel, will receive back a hundredfold (Mark 10:29–30). On the basis of this verse, we could argue for deontological conduct with a utilitarian result!

Already by saying this, I am pointing out that the distinction between utilitarianism and deontology is relative. We must consider God's commandment, but at the same time we may look ahead to the consequences of our action. When Moses presented God's commandments to the people of Israel, he indicated that keeping them would lead to *well-being*

(Deut. 6:24). The commandments themselves are by nature beneficial. We cannot talk about God's commandments with the tone of "Obey them and that's it!" As we shall see in chapter 5, these commandments secure our freedom.

Therefore, we should choose neither utilitarianism nor deontology as the basis for our ethics. Our conduct must be deontological, but never one-sidedly so. We always look at and weigh the benefit, as utilitarians do. Occasionally, tension between these two approaches can arise. Although we can gauge the benefit of many actions, both for ourselves and for others, we don't always see the benefits. We can experience an inner conflict as we seek to accept as good that which God says is good for us and for others. Respect for God, and faith that in such cases the good and the beneficial will coincide, mean that in such cases we act deontologically, believing that, from a utilitarian perspective, we will be better off.

CHRISTIAN ETHICS

I began this chapter with a clarification of the first element of my definition: ethics is reflection upon moral conduct. We were dealing quite generally with ethics. Every conceivable system of ethics considers good and evil, motivation, virtue, and values. Ethics is not an enterprise of Christians only. Recall what Paul writes in Romans 2:14–15 about pagans who show that the work of the law has been written in their hearts, and who are constantly interacting with that in their consciences, in relation both to themselves and to others.

Nevertheless, we encounter huge differences as soon as we ask what people consider to be good and evil, or *how* people are motivated, or *which* virtues and values people consider important. Apparently, people view ethical matters quite differently. We saw that already in the previous section, where we discussed concepts like utilitarianism and deontology. What people understand by "benefit," and which norms and commandments people respect, can diverge radically.

In order to clarify these differences in viewpoint, I employ in my definition the term *perspective.* We all deal frequently with the same issues, but we nevertheless look at them differently. What is the starting point for evaluating these issues? Is it the perspective, for example, of humanism, Islam, or Buddhism, or are we guided by a Christian starting point? Every system of ethical reflection lies embedded within a worldview. I owe my own worldview to the light shining from the Bible. "Your word is a lamp to my feet and a light to my path," I confess with Psalm 119:105. Therefore, ethics is for me *Christian* ethics, reflection upon moral conduct *in light of the perspective offered to us in Holy Scripture.*

Here I use the expression "Holy Scripture," but I could as well speak of "the Bible" or "the Word of God." Instead of the singular "Holy Scripture," we could as well speak of "the Holy Scriptures." For the Bible has sixty-six books, making up the Old and New Testaments. In this book, I employ the singular, even as the Bible itself does (John 10:35; 17:12; 1 Tim. 5:18). This indicates that, even though the sixty-six books display significant variety, nevertheless we are dealing with one book, about whose content Paul writes, "All Scripture is given by inspiration of God, and is profitable for doctrine, for reproof, for correction, for instruction in righteousness, that the man of God may be complete, thoroughly equipped for every good work" (2 Tim. 3:16–17). Those words of God provide leading for all our life, and surely also for our reflection upon what is good, as the verses we just quoted declare emphatically.

BIBLICAL OR CHRISTIAN ETHICS?

So we will be studying *Christian* ethics. Other titles are less suitable. Let me mention a few.

We could opt for the title "biblical ethics." But if we do that, a misunderstanding arises quickly. The Bible provides building blocks for our ethics, but the Bible itself provides no ethics that we can simply adopt as our own. That becomes clear when we pause to think about morality described in the Bible. Abraham, Moses, David, the prophets, and the apostles lived each in their own time with their own particular, occasionally varying morality. Their systems of morality contained antiquated elements, like vigilantism, polygamy, and slavery. As I now write an introduction to Christian ethics as a guide for behavior *today*, I cannot simply be led directly by what people in Bible times did or didn't do. It would be little more than descriptive ethics (see chap. 1) if I described what kind of morality people pursued in the days of Abraham, David, or Paul. But we are interested precisely in normative ethics. What is the significance of Scripture for that?

Ethics can be found in the Bible. A book like Proverbs is full of reflection upon human conduct. But we cannot adopt even its ethics as is. We live in another time, with ancient, but also modern problems. Equipped with knowledge of our own time and its questions, we must listen attentively to what the entire Scripture has to tell us. We have not reached our goal by quoting a verse from here or a text from there. In a subsequent chapter, I will explain more clearly how we should use Scripture in our ethics.

The title "theological ethics" I also find less suitable for this book. Of course, I am aware that I am writing about ethics as a theologian. But the term *theological* arouses misunderstanding. The confusion becomes clear when you put theological ethics alongside medical ethics. Theological ethics is written *by* theologians, whereas medical ethics is *for* medical professionals. Medical ethics belongs to professional ethics, but theological ethics does not, at least not to the profession of theologian and only partially to the office of minister of the Word. The ethics occupying the attention of the theologian is today usually no broader or narrower than the ethics that every Christian deals with in one way or another.

Moreover, we no longer conduct our ethical reflection in theological isolation; rather, cooperation with nontheologians who can also read the Bible has become common. For that reason, we can identify the results of our ethical reflection more clearly as Christian ethics than as theological ethics.

Literature

Aristotle. [1976] 1986. *The ethics of Aristotle: The Nicomachean ethics.* Translated by J. A. K. Thomson. Revised by Hugh Tredennick. Reprint. New York: Penguin Books.

De Graaf, J. 1972. *Verandering van de moraal.* Baarn: Bosch en Keuning.

De Graaf, J. 1986. *Elementair begrip van de ethiek.* 4th ed. Utrecht: Bohn Scheltema Holkema.

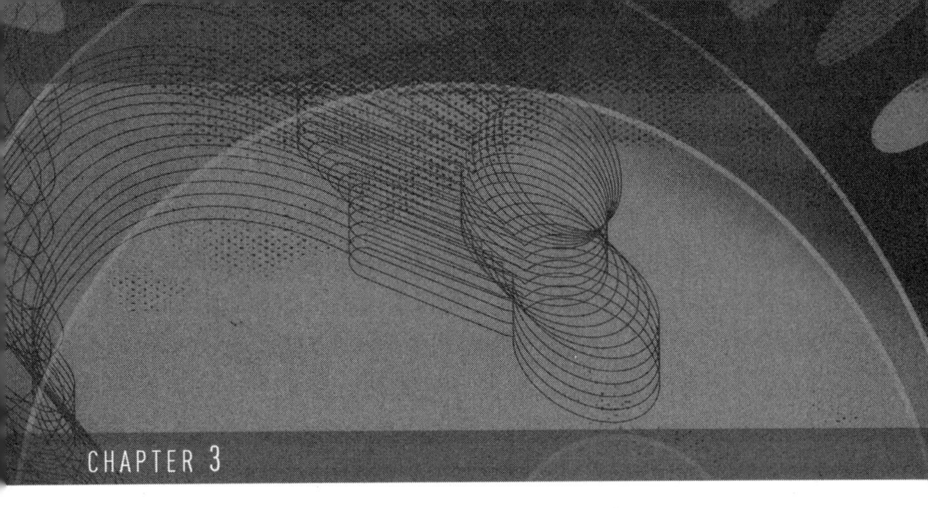

The Scope of Christian Ethics

WHY A DIFFERENT DEFINITION?

If you are familiar with an earlier edition of this introduction to ethics, entitled *Christian Morals and Ethics,* you will notice that I am now using a definition of Christian ethics that is different from the one in that book. There the definition went like this: "Ethics is reflection upon the responsible conduct of man toward God and his neighbor." The most important change is that I no longer speak of ethics as reflection upon our conduct toward *God*. That may seem rather strange for someone like me, who claims to be writing about ethics from the perspective of Scripture! All of us know that the law of God has *two* tables. The first tells us how we are to love *God,* the second how we must love our *neighbor*. Why, then, do I no longer mention God in my definition of ethics and appear to restrict my analysis of moral conduct to our relationships with other people?

Let me quiet any concerns by saying that although I no longer mention God in my definition of ethics, I will certainly be referring to Him on almost every page that follows. One who writes about ethics from the perspective of Scripture writes about God as He has revealed Himself in Jesus Christ. The word *Christian* is not being used in the phrase *Christian ethics* for decoration, to dress up our ethics with a few biblical words like *love of neighbor, compassion,* or *justice.* No, our use of the term *Christian* signifies what the whole Bible teaches by identifying Jesus Christ as the central figure. We must be clear about this. But there is something else to consider. I was impressed, as I studied earlier Reformed ethicists, that when they considered ethics and morality, they were looking at our conduct in relation to our neighbor. The relationship between people they termed "moral," but the relationship between people and God had for them a religious nature. For example, W. Geesink, who taught ethics at the Free University of Amsterdam from 1890 onward for years, spoke of a twofold service to God. We serve God *directly* by praying to Him, by praising Him, and by listening to His Word preached in church. But we serve Him *indirectly* by loving our neighbor, by honoring our parents, by respecting the life and property of our neighbor, by speaking the truth toward our neighbor, etc. So all service is service of God, whether we pray to Him or love our neighbor. But not all service is of a moral or ethical nature. That characteristic, according to Geesink, applies only to actions performed in the context of relationships among people (Geesink 1931, 2:17–20).

That distinction appears also in our own word usage. Heavy words like *sin* and *transgress* we use especially when speaking about one's relationship to God. (That word "especially" is important, since the Bible does speak in places about sinning against one's neighbor: Gen. 20:9; 40:1; 1 Sam. 2:25;

2 Chron. 6:22; Luke 15:18.) Think of Psalm 51, where after his adultery with Bathsheba, David says, "Against You, You only, have I sinned, and done this evil in Your sight" (v. 4).

When we have a conflict with people, that difficulty is an ethical one, but we don't generally speak of an ethical conflict in our relationship to God. There is a difference between religion (faith) and morality. It can happen that we differ radically from our neighbor when it comes to faith, without that difference necessarily leading to a moral conflict. In the area of politics, we can often cooperate quite well with others who do not share our faith, because we have much in common morally.

The Christian philosopher Herman Dooyeweerd distinguishes fifteen modalities or aspects of reality and classifies the moral aspect between the juridical and the pistic (or faith) aspects (1984, 2:55–163). This brings to mind what we discussed in chapter 2, where we observed that not every act is a moral act. Looking at reality in terms of a hierarchical scale of aspects, the moral aspect is located under others and above still others. The aspect just below the moral aspect is the juridical aspect of reality, which has a lot to do with morality, but is not identical to it. The aspect just above the moral aspect is the religious or faith aspect.

Seen from the perspective of the Christian faith itself, morality evidently consists of conduct toward other people, but does not coincide with our direct relationship to God. We know the biblical message that harlots and publicans, despite their wretched behavior, will nevertheless precede others in entering the kingdom of God, even though those other people have a higher moral grade. If morality were the ultimate and highest aspect of human existence, something like this would be difficult to explain. But stronger than every morality is the grace of God that makes many to be first who are last. Faith in God, who justifies the godless, preserves us from all self-exaltation, from the prayer of the Pharisee who had it together morally so much better than the publican. The publican, however, who humbled himself before God, was justified (Luke 18:14). Morality and ethics do not have the last word!

In putting it this way, I am not saying that morality and religion belong to two different worlds. We are looking at one service to God (recall what Geesink said). Even though we distinguish two tables, they constitute one law of God. Harlots and publicans do not enter the kingdom of God to remain harlots and publicans. Jesus forgives the adulterous woman, whom the Pharisees had judged to be worthy of stoning. He let her go free, but He did say, "Go and sin no more" (John 8:11).

That morality and ethics have everything to do with our relationship to God comes out in our definition when it speaks of the central position of Scripture. We deal with ethics only by proceeding from the perspective that Scripture provides for us. Ours is, after all, *Christian* ethics.

DOES IT INCLUDE THE ENVIRONMENT?

Our current definition says simply that Christian ethics is reflection upon moral conduct, nothing more. Our earlier definition described ethics as reflection upon our conduct toward God and our neighbor. I have removed this addition intentionally. One might expect, after reading the first section of this chapter, that the definition would be: Christian ethics is reflection upon moral conduct *toward other people.* But we must not draw the boundaries too tightly, as if ethics dealt only with the relationships between people. For the rest of creation is also in view. What must we think about the environment, about things, about plants and animals, all of which we must treat responsibly? If someone mistreats an animal, even if no human person is hurt thereby, is that not a moral evil? At that point, our conduct involves not our neighbor, but another creature that God has entrusted to us. In chapter 2, we insisted that the animals (including mammals) should not be viewed as our neighbors. There remains a qualitative difference between a human being and an animal. But even without viewing animals as our neighbors, because we have received a status *above* the animals (Gen. 1:26–28), we still have a moral responsibility for animals, as we do in fact for the entire natural environment in which we live. To seriously damage the environment is morally wrong not only because we thereby injure other people, or because we leave our posterity sitting with the brokenness resulting from careless environmental policies and practices. Even if we did not injure our neighbor, it is still a moral evil to treat trees, mountains, plants, and animals merely in terms of our self-interest. So morality involves our responsibility not only for people, but also for everything that is inextricably connected to the world of human beings. The environment and nature are not independent entities alongside mankind. Moral responsibility is due not only toward one's neighbor, but also toward the environment and nature.

DOES IT INCLUDE THE ACTING SUBJECT?

If we have moral responsibility toward our neighbor, do we also have this responsibility toward ourselves? Or does the subject, the "I," somehow fall outside the realm of ethics? Were such the case, it would indeed be strange to talk about motive, virtue, duty, suicide, organ transplants, and the like. After all, we are dealing continually with the experience of our own personal responsibility. Our behavior toward others is compared to what we want others to do toward us. Recall the so-called Golden Rule of Matthew 7:12: "Whatever you want men to do to you, do also to them." What you must do toward others may be deduced from the conduct we desire from others.

A distinction is made between personal and social ethics. Personal ethics reflects upon the personal life of individuals. Themes like motive, virtue, conscience, and love are discussed here. Social ethics reflects upon the structures in which people function as communal beings. Economic and political structures especially receive attention here.

The distinction between *personal* and *social* ethics is not crisp or sharp. That stands to reason. When we are dealing with social ethics, the actor is as much in view as in personal ethics. In ethics, both the neighbor and I myself are objects of attention. Reflection upon moral conduct in all sectors of human life is at the same time reflection upon ourselves.

An entirely different question is whether *love for one's neighbor* has a parallel in *self-love*. Am I commanded to love myself, as I love my neighbor? We will return to this in chapter 7, when we discuss the subject of love.

DOGMATICS AND ETHICS

In this chapter, we are busy delimiting the field of Christian ethics. What is included and what is excluded? It is useful to delimit Christian ethics also in relation to Christian dogmatics or systematic theology. Dogmatics is a characteristically theological discipline, ethics far less so. That was once different, when ethics was a theological discipline, even as dogmatics. Ethics was taught almost solely by theologians. Frequently, the disciplines of dogmatics and ethics were taught by the same person. The increasing scope of ethical issues has made the combining of these disciplines no longer possible. This disconnection is not a matter of principle, but simply a matter of the distribution of labor. Nowadays the discipline of ethics has become so diverse that it can hardly be called a theological discipline. Virtually everyone deals with ethics, and so this discipline has become far more well known than dogmatics.

What is the difference between these two disciplines? Dogmatics treats the dogmas of the church, whereas ethics deals with the life of the Christian. If alongside the dogmas of doctrine we were to speak of the dogmas of practice, then we might think of the Ten Commandments and the Sermon on the Mount as the basis for Christian living. Formerly, the word *dogma* referred both to the articles of faith (*articula fidei*) and to the precepts of the Decalogue (*praecepta decalogi*). Alongside the norm pertaining to matters to be believed, the so-called *norma credendorum,* there is the norm pertaining to matters to be done (*norma agendorum*).

In principle, it is not a problem when doctrinal and ethical perspectives are intermingled. One cannot call Calvin's *Institutes* a dogmatics or an ethics in the modern, scientific sense of those words. But we can surely see that doctrine and life are treated together from the first page to the last of the *Institutes.* The section "De vita hominis christiani" (*Institutes* 3.6–10), dealing with the life of the Christian, cannot be extracted from the rest of the *Institutes* without mutilating it. Calvin knew what every dogmatician and ethicist must know, namely, that every doctrine (in dogmatics) has an ethical side, and every ethical question roots deep in the soil of dogma. Scripture teaches that faith without works is dead, even as works without faith (James 2:14–26; Rom. 4:1–4).

To illustrate the unity of dogmatics and ethics, one ethicist compares them to a coin. The head (dogmatics) indicates the legal quality of the coin; the tail (ethics) identifies the value of the coin for practical living. Dogmatics and ethics are sides of the same coin (Van Oyen 1952, 18–19). One could also put it this way: dogmatics emphasizes correct faith, and ethics accents directed faith (Rothuizen 1973, 81).

Today we must also be conscious of the unity between dogmatics and ethics. Some forms of theology are little more than ethics. Only those truths of the Christian faith that "do something" for a person may be considered credible. Dogmas like the Trinity, Christ's deity, and the Virgin Birth don't "do" anything for people today, so they can be dropped, or else changed so radically that nothing of their original meaning remains. Ancient doctrines are evaluated in terms of their benefit. If they have none, we can let them go. This kind of viewpoint yields the result that people consider ethics far more important that dogmatics. You can accomplish something with ethics, but with dogmatics you accomplish nothing or very little anymore.

If we are to avoid reducing Christian ethics to an exercise in crass modernity, and instead go to its roots, then we will always need to return to God's revelation in Scripture and we will always bump into dogmatics or doctrine. If we limit ourselves to ethics, then we will simply be attempting to work magic with the branches, when the root of the tree has been severed, to borrow an image from Abraham Kuyper (1932, 2:346). Respect for God's broad and deep revelation, no single part of which can be comprehended apart from the whole, can preserve us from a pragmatic attitude that moves from result to truth.

Ethics is an important discipline, but God's revelation reaches far beyond talking about our conduct. To submerge dogmatics within ethics is to seek to measure God by human standards.

In the words of a variation on one of Kant's familiar expressions, one could say: Dogmatics without ethics is empty; ethics without dogmatics is blind. Dogmatics becomes arid scholasticism if its significance for living is not made clear. But ethics slides into moralism when it views our conduct apart from the work that Christ and His Spirit perform in our lives. This is expressed very well in Lord's Day 32 of the Heidelberg Catechism. There the question is asked, Why must we do good works? The answer: After having purchased us with His blood, Christ also renews us by His Holy Spirit according to His image, so that with our whole life we show ourselves thankful to God for all His benefits. This gratitude is a fruitfulness, whose fruit ripens only if the branch abides in the vine, who is Christ (John 15:1–8). Anyone writing an ethics that has room for the sanctification of living must show that this sanctification lies embedded in the liberation provided by Christ.

CHRISTIAN AND PHILOSOPHICAL ETHICS

There is yet one more important distinction that must be discussed in this chapter. We want to write about Christian ethics, but how does Christian ethics relate to philosophical ethics? Earlier in this chapter, I wrote that in former times ethics was primarily the business of theologians. But we should also note that ethics has always been part of philosophy as well. As you page through histories of philosophy, you will notice that writers of such works often write about the ideas a philosopher had about ethics.

The distinction between Christian ethics and philosophical ethics is often put this way: philosophical ethics proceeds from the fact of morality itself; Christian ethics proceeds from Scripture and the divine command found there. Philosophical ethics is supposedly autonomous; Christian ethics is heteronomous.

For example, Immanuel Kant presented a philosophical ethics in his *Critique of Practical Reason.* What is remarkable is that in his ethics Kant accepts the premises that there is life after death and that God exists. That doesn't seem very autonomous, and we might suppose that Kant borrowed this from Scripture. But in his own opinion, Kant arrived at these conclusions strictly on the basis of rational reflection. He called the existence of God and the immortality of man *postulates,* to indicate that we must accept the existence of God and the continuation of man, even though these cannot be proved in the same way we can prove that the sum of the angles in a triangle is 180 degrees. Kant believed that with understanding or reason he could demonstrate the existence of God and the immortality of man on the basis of the fact of morality itself and not on the basis of God's revelation in Scripture. However, other philosophers who deal with ethics never arrive at a postulate about the existence of God or the immortality of man. Kant's conclusion regarding the immortality of the soul had everything to do with the echoes of the Christian faith in which he was nurtured and to which he could not possibly close his ears, even though he was seeking to construct an ethics strictly on the basis of reason.

Every ethics, Christian or non-Christian, proceeds from presuppositions. There is no such thing as "pure" reason—not even in the sense that there exists a kind of lower story where everybody should be able to reach identical conclusions in areas like ethics and politics, while the upper story of religious opinions is where division occurs. This is how Roman Catholic theology views philosophical ethics, like a kind of lower story where universal agreement is possible, while Christian ethics belongs to the upper story, where alone it is valid. Reason is universal among people; faith is not.

But "philosophical" ethics and "Christian" ethics are not two levels existing hierarchically together, like "nature" (lower story) and "grace" (upper story). The Christian faith is determinative for everything, from the foundation to the roof. When 2 Corinthians 10:5 speaks of "bringing every thought into captivity to the obedience of Christ," then reason is pure only when it has been won to Christ.

In principle, therefore, there is no dilemma requiring us to choose between Christian ethics and philosophical ethics. The philosopher too must submit to God's revelation. There is certainly a difference in defining problems and in methodology between philosophy and theology. But the philosopher and the theologian do not live in separate worlds, one where the former works without faith, another where the theologian proceeds from faith.

Both Christian ethics and philosophical ethics register fundamental conclusions about man. Ethics too bumps into the question of anthropology. Our definition mentions reflection upon human moral conduct. A brief description of two kinds of anthropology can clarify how each yields a different kind of ethics. I have in mind a rather widespread modern anthropology leading to one kind of ethics, over against which I put a Christian anthropology with its resulting ethics.

Many contend that the phenomenon of morality results from the evolution of man from an animal. An animal is understood to be a preprogrammed being. An animal is characterized by the limited number of behavioral alternatives that to a large extent are fixed, and by its well-developed instincts. In terms of its behavior, an animal has it rather easy, you might say. But with people it is different. A human being is, says Arnold Gehlen, a *Mängelwesen,* which means "a being with shortcomings." Unlike animals, people do not live in their own preprogrammed little world, but must construct their world themselves. A person must choose from a number of possibilities, since he acts instinctively only to a very limited degree. Choosing from an unlimited number of possibilities is so difficult that it becomes necessary to *limit* that number. That is what morality is concerned about. Morality offers a limited number of rules of conduct that relieve people of the need to weigh and determine, every time anew, what should and should not be done. For example, marriage is a relationship of commitment to one partner. We don't need to look repeatedly for a new partner. Such a permanent relationship can contribute to security and stability. One can use the creativity and energy saved thereby for doing other things. Morality cannot remain the same forever, for when an accepted morality begins to work in a way that constricts rather than liberates, then we need to abandon it. After all, morality aims at the development of the person. The human person is the center of morality.

In contrast to this philosophical vision of man and his morality, I would posit the Christian confession that understands man not as an evolved *Mängelwesen*, but as a creature of God, created according to God's image. Not man, but God stands at the center, because from Him and through Him and unto Him are all things (Rom. 11:36). Man has God and not himself as his lawgiver.

Here the characteristic difference between humanistic philosophical ethics and Christian ethics appears most clearly: it is not I who determine what does or does not serve my freedom, for God's commandment has determined that for me. Imagine that someone sees his marriage as broken and seeks relief in a relationship with another woman. He may perhaps experience that as liberating, but it surely is not liberating for someone who accepts the seventh commandment as God's precept: "Thou shalt not commit adultery."

We see the difference between both kinds of ethics also when we recall what was said about utilitarianism back in chapter 2. Often morality is weighed in terms of its benefit or profitability. If it serves people's interests, then it is beneficial. If not, then it should be thrown overboard. Moral rules must bring humanity to further development, or they simply obstruct such development. For example, it used to be that premarital and extramarital sexual relations were forbidden, but today people need room for free sexual expression. The ancient sexual morality has become injurious, because it no longer adequately answers the needs of modern man.

To be sure, Christian ethics doesn't dispense with the word *utilitarian*, as we have already seen. But what is really beneficial? If our horizon extends no farther than the limits of this brief earthly life, then we too would perhaps choose a humanistic ethics, one that tries to make the best of this life. But Scripture says that piety is profitable "for all things, having promise of the life that now is and of that which is to come" (1 Tim. 4:8). We must not put on blinders with regard to this! Even though we sense that obedience to God's commandment seems to yield no profit for the short term, we should still not doubt that it will in the long term. The self-denial that God asks of us is not self-destruction, but truly leads us to full self-development, as we have already observed. Within the limited horizon of this life, self-denial could often be said to be entirely unprofitable. But it is profitable for someone who makes his decisions in faith within a broader horizon. For there is yet another life after this one, when it will be clear, if it has not yet become clear in this life, that God's good commandment was also a profitable commandment.

You see, the ways part in our respective anthropologies. But the separation is not between a neutral, objective philosophy and ethics, on the one hand, and a Christian, subjective religion and ethics, on the other. Nothing in the arena of worldviews is neutral, and the same holds true for philosophy. There the line of separation runs between non-Christian and Christian philosophies. Is man autonomous, so that he himself determines the law, or is he heteronomous, because he stands under God's commandment?

To many ears, the word *heteronomous* sounds terrible. That is understandable enough, because they see their own freedom endangered when we insist that we stand under the command of another. But that Other is God Himself, who established the law not to bind our life in chains, but precisely to bring it to unfolding maturity. Here, binding means freedom. True freedom listens to God's laws.

I have provided an example of two kinds of anthropology that are opposed to each other. Others could be offered. But in each case, this is true: show me your philosophical view of man, and I will show you what ethics you subscribe to. Some view man as a free being who can choose from a number of possibilities; others view him as a being who is determined and entirely unfree, who acts out of necessity. Some people see man as a being determined by his body. Feelings and desires are not governed by reason, but instead they govern reason (materialistic ethics). Marxist ethics posits that man is conditioned entirely by economic relationships. This kind of ethics is rarely defended any longer today. But not everything said in Marxist ethics was mistaken. Man is in fact determined by quite a few factors. Anyone who sings loudly about man's freedom of choice will quickly lower his volume when he looks around a bit. Most people inhabiting this globe are far from free, since their lives are prescribed and circumscribed in any number of ways.

Moreover, being heteronomous (subject to the law of another) is no shame for mankind, as we have already observed. The big question is, Under whom do you stand or place yourself? Those who bow before God and His law may say that they are free and that their existence is truly humane in the fullest sense of the word.

WITH UNIVERSAL AND WITH CHRISTIAN ARGUMENTS

At this point, it might seem that we wish to avoid contact with philosophical ethics, or at least with non-Christian philosophical ethics. But that is incorrect. I indicated earlier that a difference in faith does not yet signify a resulting simultaneous difference in morality. This means that we may expect to learn from philosophical ethics, even if it does not proceed from a fundamentally Christian conviction. We have and hold much in common as human beings. For that reason, within Christian ethics we cannot limit ourselves over against philosophical ethics in such a way that we employ only Christian arguments, whereas philosophical ethics uses only universal arguments. We need both Christian and universal arguments.

When I speak of *universal* arguments, I am referring to arguments that all of us, regardless of our religious differences, can employ in order to reach a consensus on ethical subjects. Involved here is moral discussion using *rational* arguments, a discussion in which everybody can participate without having to appeal to special—in this case, Christian—arguments. Such discussions often involve issues of justice and especially of injustice. All of us have a sense of what constitutes injustice and discrimination. In our world, a large number of human rights have been clearly formulated and universal arguments accepted in the struggle against gross injustice. The rule of thumb, "What you do not wish others to do to you, don't do to another," is familiar to everybody. It appears not only in Scripture, but also in other cultures. More than once we have had the experience that a non-Christian using this rule of thumb has unmasked injustice in the world, often more clearly than Christians have. In this light, a person like Nelson Mandela has meant more for the dismantling of apartheid than all the Reformed believers put together, who with a few exceptions defended the apartheid regime too long, even with the use of Bible verses.

Now, of course, ethics deals with more subjects than simply justice and injustice. I am thinking not strictly of countering injustice, but of showing care, sympathy, compassion, and love. Are we prepared to exert ourselves on behalf of our needy neighbor, even when nobody has the right to rule our pocketbooks or our time? Are we prepared to do more than what we are by duty obligated to do? Christians confronted with these questions cannot but think of Jesus and His devotion to poor, sick, and rejected people. When others appeal to us to exert ourselves on behalf of our neighbor next door or far away, we will always be confronted with our Christian motivation. Surely this constitutes a self-evident Christian component of our discussion. If someone must do something for his poor neighbor, then surely that befits us who are Christians. *Noblesse oblige* (noble people must behave nobly). We have in mind here issues like care for the sick and aged, fighting poverty, or even organ donation.

Nevertheless, all these actions can be found just as prominently among non-Christians, and occasionally even—again, to our shame—more prominently than among us who are Christians. Along with *justice, love* is neither an exclusively Christian word nor an exclusively Christian matter. The motivations may differ, but the result of showing love is often the same. Once more we recognize that many issues, discussed in the context of fruitful consultation within our pluriform society, can lead to shared conclusions and actions, regardless of the difference between Christian and non-Christian motivations.

Is this all we can say? Many ethicists, also in the Christian camp, believe it is. They consider it very worthwhile to talk about the Christian *motivation* of moral conduct. But this difference in motivation does not obstruct the route we need to travel toward communal action. Together we must and we can continue constructing the morality of our political society. Precisely because that moral commonality exists, they believe that there are no *activities* and *patterns of conduct* that can be stamped as distinctively Christian. We can continue discussing any and every moral issue in terms of universal arguments. All of us need to stay at the same table, using universal arguments to clarify our differences, and we all need to keep on striving for communal action. Universality dominates the ethical arena. Each has his or her own faith? Fine, but each must aim at the same solution for action.

Unfortunately, such a description of the situation is too optimistic. One clear example of this is the issue of euthanasia. Here it won't work to advance only universal arguments. Consider the patient who, on his own and in consultation with his immediate family, makes the self-conscious and sustained decision to request euthanasia. In his view, the concluding stage of his life is characterized only by suffering and humiliation, and is completely empty of meaning. What can I say in response? Who can make it clear with universal arguments to someone who begins with *the right of self-determination*, that he must continue living when he will experience nothing but a hard life, when his family is willing to facilitate his easy death, and when a physician is prepared to administer that death? However, the situation is completely different when we begin, not with the right of self-determination, but rather understand the course of our lives to be in God's hand. God called us into this life. He calls us out of this life, at His time and not ours. What moves someone who is dying in Christ not to request euthanasia I cannot articulate in universal arguments.

So it comes down to this: we employ a *Christian* argument against doing what others do as the consistent outworking of their non-Christian starting point, namely, determine the moment of death themselves. (For an expanded discussion of the "universal" and "Christian" arguments used in the discussion of euthanasia, see Douma 1997, 267–79.)

I have used the example of euthanasia because everyone can see clearly that this issue has not only personal but also public aspects, such that it always reappears on the political agenda. But more issues could be mentioned, issues in which it is clear that Christian arguments play a role, even a decisive role, in accepting or rejecting things judged by today's society as morally acceptable. You need look only at the various expressions of sexual lifestyles, both heterosexual and homosexual, or at current opinions about marriage in connection with using modern medical technology for either obtaining or preventing progeny. So we are dealing not simply with differing motivations that may nonetheless lead to identical actions, but with differing motivations that *exclude* common action. It generally comes down to the question Do we ourselves govern our own lives? Or do we live in dependence upon God, who has provided laws for that life? Here faith and action are seamlessly woven together so that one can hardly expect a communal public morality.

Of course, we must always examine ourselves in this matter. We can cut off discussion too quickly, supposing that trying to come to agreement with others by means of universal arguments is pointless. The Dutch theologian K. Schilder once wrote that the law of God is the only garment that truly fits the world. If that is so, and if listening to the laws of God allows human life to blossom, whereas not listening to them is harmful to mankind, we will be able to demonstrate this with universal arguments as well. As the proverb says, you know the tree by its fruit, sour or sweet. Therefore, we should not claim too quickly that there are no universal arguments available by which to distinguish good from evil. Does not Scripture itself show us, in a book like Proverbs, that when we or others disregard laws for living, such disregard is not only sinful, but especially stupid? It is not pointless for us, really, to make plain by means of universal arguments that it is good for a person to rest one day each week, to respect the authority of parents and of others, to keep our hands off the life and property of our neighbor, and to speak the truth. When we illumine prudence and stupidity using the Ten Commandments, we are showing the profit and benefit of these commandments. Recall what we discussed in chapter 2. A Christian ethicist is not the kind of deontologist who says, "Listen to God's commandments, and that's it." He may also be a utilitarian and say, "Listen to God's commandments and you will see what is really profitable for you."

So we can go a long way with universal arguments; but they have their limits, as I have tried to make clear. We need both kinds of arguments. And it seems obvious that we can learn much from philosophical ethics—both Christian and non-Christian—in using universal arguments.

After all, Christian ethics is more than providing good counsel to Christians within the church. Christian ethics must also be aimed at serving public society in its analysis of the prevailing general morality and in its approval and criticism of this morality. Christians must be able to communicate with universal arguments and not retreat too quickly to the rear lines, where we defend positions only with Christian arguments. Often precisely those universal arguments inform people most clearly that it is good and profitable for morality to keep God's commandments.

Christian ethics can also bring to light the fact that both Christian and non-Christian ethicists are driven by their faith. When others believe that *they themselves* govern their own lives, that is as much of a faith commitment as the belief that *God* governs our lives. The enormous influence exerted in modern society by the belief in self-determination easily blinds our eyes, giving us the impression that the appeal to self-governance is an appeal to a universal argument. But such an appeal is not driven any less by faith than the Christian argument that not we ourselves, but God, governs the course of life and death.

How do we know that? For that we appeal to Scripture. I formulated my definition of Christian ethics as reflection upon moral conduct in light of the perspective offered to us in Holy Scripture. It is now time to devote some discussion to the last part of my definition. We employ Scripture in our ethics. But how should we do that?

Literature

Geesink, W. 1931. *Gereformeerde ethiek.* 2 vols. Kampen: Kok.

Dooyeweerd, Herman. 1984. *A new critique of theoretical thought.* Translated by David H. Freeman and H. de Jongste. 4 vols. St. Catharines, Ont.: Paideia.

Douma, J. 1997. *Medische ethiek.* Kampen: Kok.

Kuyper, A. 1932. *De gemeene gratie.* 3d ed. Kampen: Kok.

Rothuizen, G. Th. 1973. *Wat is ethiek?* Kampen: Kok.

Van Oyen, H. 1952. *Evangelische Ethik. Grundlagen.* Basel: Reinhardt.

CHAPTER 4

THE USE OF HOLY SCRIPTURE

DIFFICULTIES

If we believe that Christian ethics is possible, then we will have to flesh out that word *Christian* with some content. Why do we consider one thing to be Christian and not another thing? To answer that, we must have a norm, a rule according to which we measure what is and what is not Christian.

The word *norm* is derived from the Latin word *norma*, which originally meant "a carpenter's square," an instrument used to determine whether a corner is square and straight. The norm is the guideline, the measuring tool, the rule whereby we evaluate whether something is straight and right or not.

So then, the norm for Christian ethics we find in Holy Scripture. There God has revealed what is good and what He expects of us (Mic. 6:8). God's Word is a lamp for my feet and a light upon my path (Ps. 119:105). That Word is profitable for teaching, for rebuking, for correcting, and for training in righteousness, "that the man of God may be complete, thoroughly equipped for every good work" (2 Tim. 3:16–17).

But difficulties arise at this point. Many people appeal to Scripture to justify their conduct. But they don't all do so in the same way. The most contradictory positions have been and are defended with an appeal to what we find in Scripture. Submission to the government and revolution against authority have both been defended. The right to private property and the right of confiscation have been similarly defended. Proponents and opponents of the homosexual lifestyle appeal to Scripture. Is determining who is right a hopeless business, then? What is left of using Scripture as our norm?

Our answer to this question must be that Scripture is misused in numerous ways, but that misuse does not vitiate its proper use. If you consider appealing to Scripture to have little merit because there are always people who use Scripture to defend contradictory positions, then you must also realize that this is not a modern phenomenon. In their use of Scripture, the Pharisees opposed Jesus and the Judaizers opposed Paul, but neither Jesus nor Paul ever let the Scriptures lie unused because of that. The apostle Peter realized that the letters of Paul contained some difficult passages, but at the same time he criticized the "untaught and unstable" who twisted not only these letters, but the rest of the Scriptures "to their own destruction" (2 Peter 3:15–16). Holy Scripture, inspired by God (2 Tim. 3:16), remains the Word of God, no matter how many hands defile it.

A second difficulty lies in the historical character of Scripture. The Bible shows us the progressive history of God's redemption through Jesus Christ. The coming of Jesus changed many things, such that not everything God once commanded His people Israel in the course of that history remains valid. We might think, for example, of the sacrifices that were to be rendered, or of the agriculturally flavored legislation, or the ceremonial festivals, or the various strict punishments for various crimes—all of these contained in the Mosaic legislation.

Not everything in force during the time of Moses and the prophets remains in force now in the New Testament period. But that confronts us with another question: What is and is not in force now? What parts of the Mosaic legislation continue in force, and what parts were temporary?

Yet a third difficulty confronts us. Many ethical questions involve modern developments that were unknown in Bible times. In fact, how many subjects requiring our attention in ethics today were unknown even one hundred years ago? How must we decide about limiting the size of our family with the help of the Pill or sterilization? How must we decide about nuclear weapons, organ transplants, or test-tube babies? Simply reaching for a Bible text won't work here.

Does Scripture have a message for us in such situations, then, and if so, how do we discover it?

HERMENEUTICS

In this chapter we are seeking to answer such questions. As we look for those answers, we are involved in what is called hermeneutics. The word *hermeneutics* comes from the Greek word *hermēneuō*, meaning "to translate." How should we interpret Scripture when we seek its judgment in our ethical reflection? How must we deal with the Bible if we want to know what moral conduct God requires of us today?

In speaking of hermeneutics, I am starting with the early usage of this concept. I believe that the church of Christ, led by the Spirit of God, is in a position to apply God's Word. We don't read the Bible by ourselves, individualistically, but together "with all the saints" (Eph. 3:18). So our personal Bible reading does not start with an empty slate. As soon as we ourselves read Scripture with self-awareness and inquire as to what we must do in this or that situation, we are already standing in a tradition of Bible interpretation and application that we follow for the most part. The Bible has been applied before, and it is obvious that in numerous instances we will find that application acceptable.

When we do, we are not thereby putting Scripture as the Word of God on the same level as the tradition of Bible interpretation. But for that reason this tradition is very important. Nobody can live without tradition, including the tradition of interpreting the Bible. If we had to do things without any tradition, then we would have to discover and invent everything ourselves. To rely upon the correctness of Bible interpretation within the church, where the Word of God has been heard with respect, is to rely upon the leading of God's Spirit, who has been promised to the church (John 14:15ff.). For that reason, it is not hard to recognize our own reflection in the lifestyle of Christians who lived in those early centuries. Although our morality is different from that of David, we don't live in such a radically different world that David looks foreign to us when we take note of his life and his psalms. Augustine wrote very negatively about human sexuality, something we should not imitate. But it is not at all difficult for a confessing Christian to feel more at home with the church father Augustine than with many moderns who call themselves Christian but defend the permissibility of sexual pleasure before and beyond marriage. Calvin practiced a strict discipline in Geneva, but his practice displayed more of the law and the gospel than is evident in the life of a modern Western "Christian" city today. It is true that much has changed (see below), but much has also remained the same. Otherwise we would be unable to recognize ourselves in the lives of Christians who lived in the early church, the Middle Ages, and the time of the Reformation, a recognition I have just been illustrating.

But I must add something immediately. The history of morality shows us that many mistakes have been made. Apparently we can err rather seriously even when we declare that this or that is God's will for us. I have clarified this already. Tradition has great value, but we must not become traditionalists, who say that we must do something because that's what our grandparents did. It is true that we need not discover for the first time the meaning of Scripture for our morality, but we must indeed rediscover that meaning again and again. Nothing stays the same, and much of the past that was fine has been lost. If the church suffers apostasy, then that is a catastrophe not only for good doctrine, but for good living as well. If the Word of God is no longer purely and powerfully preached, we may expect that the Christian life will suffer damage from that. But if we turn a blind eye to new developments in life in order to keep everything the way it was, then that too will cause damage. For then we are forgetting that a new period in history generates new questions requiring answers. Consider, for example, questions being addressed to ethics in terms of developments in technology (nuclear weapons, genetic engineering, etc.). Alongside the old, whose value we must examine and test, is the new, which we need to evaluate as to whether it is wholesome or injurious. We believe in the leading of the Holy Spirit, but that leading does not bring our own activity to a standstill.

No matter how thankful we must be for the insights that the hermeneutics of former generations provide us, we must always make that tradition our own, at times supplementing or even correcting it. Hermeneutics guides us in using Scripture well, putting us in a position to evaluate our own ideas critically.

There are other kinds of hermeneutics. This subject is far too complex to provide a thorough discussion of it in this introduction to ethics. But you can understand how it differs significantly whether one's hermeneutic starts with the confession that Scripture is the Word of God, or with a shrug of the shoulders about this presupposition. In the latter case, one will not believe that people throughout history could have and should have possessed a fundamentally similar understanding of Scripture under the leading of the Spirit of God.

Modern hermeneutics can operate in quite a different way. The starting point is not what God says, but who we ourselves are. It is oriented toward human self-understanding. The issue is not what the text—spoken in the past and valid for today—says precisely, but whether that text can be interpreted so that it touches me.

An illustration can help us here. People may no longer believe in Christ's physical resurrection from the grave, or in His ascension or return, because (as people say) a modern person can no longer take these things literally, but they can still try to interpret the relevant texts in such a way that they still have something to tell us. Christ's resurrection does indeed contain a message, but always and only within the parameters of what modern man can "relate to." Believing in a literal resurrection of a corpse out of a grave no longer fits those parameters. So then, we need to look for other interpretive possibilities that do fit what is acceptable to modern man.

The same applies to the commands in Scripture. Today it seems so old-fashioned to object to a homosexual lifestyle. But Scripture clearly disapproves of homosexual conduct. What then must we do if we don't want to ignore Scripture, and still want to give it a place in our ethics? We can interpret those texts that prohibit homosexuality in such a way that this kind of prohibition was meaningful once upon a time for human development, but is no longer relevant. For example, homosexuality supposedly conflicted with the necessary growth of Israel's population, something no longer true today. In fact, our problem today is overpopulation, which can serve as a basis for recommending homosexual conduct! For that reason, say defenders of homosexual behavior, Scripture does not reject modern forms of homosexual friendship—though it does reject every form of debauchery, like that found in Sodom (Gen. 19) and in the world of Romans 1:24–32.

In this way, Scripture is made suitable to modern man. The Bible must fit modern man, rather than modern man being made to fit the Bible. What is decisive is our human preunderstanding (German, *Vorverständnis*). One comes to Scripture with particular opinions that one does not then abandon. If in our day it is no longer possible to hold to the physical resurrection of Jesus, then all the biblical data dealing with his resurrection, taken together, does not have the power to overcome this modern view. And if a particular moral conviction, say, favoring homosexuality, has taken over, then all the biblical data about marriage and sexuality lacks the power to overcome this modern view. Such a hermeneutic can no longer permit Scripture to speak critically to modern man. Underlying this fact is the conviction that in Scripture we supposedly find, not divine revelation, but religious human experience. That experience changes over time, and along with it our view of what in Scripture is acceptable.

I mentioned earlier that hermeneutics is a complex subject. It would not be superfluous to draw attention to the fact that not everybody who approaches Scripture with the presupposition that in the Bible we find the Word of God thereby comes to the same conclusions regarding interpreting the Bible. Even in orthodox Reformed circles, there are differences of opinion (see Loonstra 1994 and Wierenga 1996). Honesty compels us to acknowledge that all of us approach Scripture with a preunderstanding. Such a preunderstanding does not operate only among those who oppose the authority of Scripture. All of us have our views about morality before we open the Bible. And the most serious mistakes that have been made in Christian morality show us all too clearly that such preunderstanding has not been entirely Christian, even though it has been clothed in Christian garb.

So all of us come to Scripture with our own presuppositions. But the issue is whether we are willing to surrender our preunderstanding if Scripture compels us to, or whether ultimately we are going to permit our preunderstanding to dominate Scripture. The Bible requires that we be converted, also when it comes to interpreting Scripture faithfully and not twisting it to fit our viewpoint. But then, conversion is possible only if we are willing to submit to the authority of God's Spirit, fully acknowledging the fallibility of our own preunderstanding. Our rejection of modern hermeneutics offers no guarantee that we will therefore always permit Scripture to tell us what God wants to tell us. In the following section, I will be discussing biblicism, something many Christians have been and still are practicing. A person can with all uprightness put himself under the authority of God's Word and still fall into the error of turning the Bible into a megaphone for his own ideas. Such a person finds his own conduct so self-evidently right that he simply cannot imagine that God's Word condemns it. And already at that point one is reading out of Scripture what one has already stuffed into it.

BIBLICISM

What do we understand by biblicism? Biblicism is the use of Scripture texts in an atomistic or isolated way. Texts are torn from their contexts. Attention is not given to the time and circumstances that provide a text with its particular tone and color. Biblicism easily places an equal sign between conduct then and conduct now. In this way, Scripture becomes a book of various examples, which come to be applied in a framework such as: Just as they did things then, so too must we do things now.

Let me provide several examples of a biblicistic use of Scripture.

William Perkins (1558–1602) thought that with an appeal to Genesis 41:42 (Joseph was clothed by Pharaoh with linen garments) he could warn his contemporaries that they should be clothed with garments befitting their own social class (1642, 333–34). He complained that the tradesman wanted to be clothed like an esquire, the esquire like a nobleman, the nobleman like a count, and the count like a prince. Such behavior would break down the order that God had assigned to people within the various social classes. Just read Genesis

41:42! The same author condemned wearing foreign clothes on the basis of Zephaniah 1:8, where it says that God will punish the princes and the king's children and all that are clothed with foreign apparel.

Concerning frills and finery, Tertullian considered it improper for women to wear hairpieces made from someone else's hair. For does not Matthew 6:27 say that we may not add to our length? Nor may we in an artificial manner add to our weight. Women do that by allowing "some kind of rolls, or shield-bosses, to be piled upon [their] necks" (*On the Apparel of Women* 2.7).

Now we can chuckle about Tertullian's advice. But there are still people who argue that girls should not wear slacks, for Deuteronomy 22:5 clearly states that a woman may not wear men's clothes, and a man may not wear women's clothing.

Not only the area of clothing, but also the area of social relationships provides samples of biblicism. The curse of Ham (Gen. 9:25) has been used numerous times to maintain slavery (especially of the blacks). The eight-hour workday has been opposed with Jesus' words that we must work as long as it is day (John 9:4), since there are twelve hours in a day (John 11:9). The five-day workweek supposedly contradicts the commandment that we must work for six days (Ex. 20:9). Nationalization of land has in former times been rejected with a cautionary appeal to Ahab's conduct toward Naboth, who refused to release his vineyard—an inheritance from his father—to King Ahab (1 Kings 21). Some have argued that an employees' union is unnecessary when we observe that Boaz sustained a good relationship with his employees without that kind of union (Ruth 2). The right of employers to oppose such an employees' union has been defended by appealing to the master of the vineyard in Matthew 20:15, who says, "Is it not lawful for me to do what I wish with my own things?"

We could go on giving examples of biblicism. Christian families have opposed playing with dice because Proverbs 16:33 supposedly teaches that the lot is holy and inappropriate for games: "The lot is cast into the lap, but its every decision is from the LORD." To this day, blood sausage is taboo for some, since Acts 15:20 commands us to abstain "from things strangled, and from blood."

Now it is rather easy to grin about these examples from the past. But there are also modern forms of biblicism in ethics. On the basis of Jesus' cleansing of the temple, people have proclaimed Him to be the great revolutionary. Theologians influenced by Marxism have equated His turning over the tables of the moneychangers with overturning political and economic structures today. Just as Amos railed against the rich in his day (Amos 5:11; 6:3ff.; 8:4ff.), so we today should condemn capitalism. Israel's year of Jubilee saw the release of debtors, which some interpret today as a protest against the rights of the powerful, or against the institution of monarchy, with its army, police, and bureaucracy.

Both forms of biblicism, in fact, are guilty of putting into Scripture what they then pull out of it. People put into the Bible prescriptions that happen to be in force in their own day, whether about social classes or appropriate clothing, in order then to "discover" those prescriptions in Scripture. Bible texts provide the imprimatur for one's own views. If someone believes that it's high time to change the existing situation, then "proof" for that need is found in Scripture.

We need not pursue further analysis of the mistakes made in the examples mentioned above. We can suffice with a few comments that signal the recurring fundamental error: using Scripture atomistically, whereby one ignores the context, the time, and the circumstances that must be taken into account in connection with the verse being quoted.

Critics of the practice of girls wearing slacks cannot appeal to Deuteronomy 22:5. That text is dealing with a religious practice in pagan Canaan, where men and women exchanged clothing as part of committing sexual immorality. A verse whose background is one of rampant licentiousness and unchastity cannot be automatically applied to a woman or a girl today who wants to wear slacks to keep warm in cold weather. Similarly, it is altogether different for a non-American to wear a T-shirt sporting the logo of Kansas State University than for someone in Zephaniah's day to wear exotic clothes advertising an exotic religion.

Our clocks do indeed measure each day in twelve-hour segments, but nowhere does the Bible say that we must work at our jobs for twelve hours each day. If you think about the free time the Israelites could enjoy with their weekly Sabbath, the Sabbath year, and the various festival weeks and days, you will certainly not conclude that our eight-hour workday is an impermissible luxury.

Ham was cursed, but if we believe on the basis of Scripture that the gospel must be brought also to black Africans, then we cannot keep them in social, political, or economic servitude. That contradicts genuine brotherhood. The Israelites were not slaves to each other, but only to God (Ex. 13:3; 19:44; Lev. 25:42; 26:13). This belief automatically led, sooner or later, to the suspension of slavery. Since, with the passing of time, slavery and colonialism have become egregious, no Christian can legitimately appeal to Scripture to maintain these practices.

Nationalizing property without regard to the right of private property is wrong. But one cannot legitimately appeal to the history of Naboth to reject nationalizing property, especially not in a society where a few wealthy property owners live among an impoverished populace.

Our ancestors viewed casting the lot as something very special. But it seems rather clear, on the basis of Proverbs 16:33, that lots can be seen as something quite ordinary—just as ordinary as thinking about which way we're going to walk (Prov. 16:9), how we are going to plant our footsteps (Prov. 20:24), seeing the sprouting of grass and foliage for man and animals (Ps. 104:14), seeing a sparrow fall to the ground, or seeing but one hair fall from your head (Matt. 10:29–20). Precisely in these ordinary things, Scripture says, we must see God's leading. So must we, too, in the outcome of tossing a pair of dice. But we need not for that reason forbid playing games that use dice.

Christians who had come out of paganism were not to eat blood, to avoid injuring their Jewish partners in faith. But the time came in the history of the church when eating blood sausage or food involved in idol sacrifices (1 Cor. 8:1ff.) no longer aroused encumbering associations with Old Testament blood sacrifices or pagan temples. So it is that today we are able to tour a Roman Catholic cathedral, even though we oppose Roman Catholic teaching, and even though such an edifice perhaps reminds us of the time when Protestant Christians were led to the stake.

We can indeed cite verses from Amos that criticize economic abuses and distressing contrasts between rich and poor. But the words of Amos and of Jesus simultaneously summon people to give their hearts to God. For them, social and economic abuses were at the same time religious abuses. So we must always point out the vertical dimension. We cut the heart out of Scripture if we omit God and conversion to God from our arguments.

TRANSITION WITHIN SCRIPTURE

We can identify a clear shift within Scripture itself that we must take into account if we want to use Scripture in ethics. We are dealing with the Old and New Testaments. In the New Testament dispensation, many Old Testament regulations are no longer in force. Peter was shown clearly that he could eat things that for him used to be unclean (Acts 10:9ff.). With respect to eating and drinking, and to festivals, new moons, and sabbaths, all of which functioned as shadowy figures of the reality of Christ, Christians were permitted more leeway than was possible for the Jews (Col. 2:16–17). When salvation extended no longer only to the Jews, but also to non-Jews throughout the world, it became obvious that the Old Testament, with its social and economic regulations, lost its force *as legislation.* We might think here of the distribution and purchasing of land, the rights and liberties of slaves, the penal sanctions, and the form of government.

Because the books of the Old Testament nonetheless retained their authority together with those of the New Testament in all the churches, it was natural that over time a distinction came to be applied to the Old Testament laws, between what remained in force and what did not. That led to the distinction between three kinds of laws: ceremonial, civil, and moral.

The *ceremonial* laws related to the temple ministry, to

matters clean and unclean, to sacrifices and other matters. These laws found their fulfillment in Christ and thus could be seen as no longer in force, even though knowledge of them continues to be valuable for understanding what we now possess in Christ.

The *civil* laws, oriented as they were to the life of the ancient covenant people in the land of Canaan, were no longer in force for Christians living in other lands. These laws did not come back into force as an integrated system of legislation even when the world had become Christianized. Deep respect for these civil laws as legislation has continued to the present day. But they could not be copied in the life of any other society, since they were far too intricately woven into the land and nation of Israel.

Finally, the *moral* laws, whose core is the Ten Commandments, have always remained in force, even for today. In these laws, we are dealing with the constant principles that remain in force, not only in the old covenant, but also in the new.

The distinction between ceremonial, civil, and moral laws is an artificial distinction. No Israelite would have made such a distinction. The Israelite and his land, with its tabernacle or temple, with its structures of government and statutes for punishment, had but one law, naturally. Making these distinctions became necessary and legitimate at the time when there was no longer any need for a temple and no possibility of living in Canaan.

But it is difficult to identify precisely what it is in these three kinds of laws that remains in force. Both the ceremonial and the civil laws remain significant for Christian ethics. We need to seek the substance, the core, of these laws. For example, most Christians no longer observe the form of fasting. Yet the heart of the matter, having to do with a person's humbling himself before God, does continue in force. We can no longer observe the sabbatical year or the year of Jubilee, but what God wanted to impress upon His people in those days by means of such laws remains valid for today, namely, that He is the one who governs the harvests and owns the land. The message that God is concerned not only with people and their social relationships, but with the land and with animals as well, is as relevant today as it was back then. So we must be careful when we say that the ceremonial and civil laws are no longer in force. Such a comment is true insofar as such laws cannot simply be copied over and enforced today. But it is not true that we have nothing more to do with those laws. What those laws teach concerning God's relationship to people and to nature continues to be relevant and meaningful.

When we take into account the shift that has occurred within Scripture in moving from the Old to the New Testament, we are taking into account *salvation history*. There is but one history that leads to Jesus Christ. And when He arose from the dead, a new age began, one that requires new conduct. Temple, land, and sacrifice all communicated a message that found its fulfillment in Christ, and therefore could not be communicated in the old forms. We need to remember that in ethics. We are trying to express that by means of the threefold distinction mentioned above, between ceremonial, civil, and moral laws. We will see later that the fulfillment in Christ of these laws given in Scripture has still more profound significance.

The Dutch theologian Klaas Schilder (1890–1952) offered a definition of ethics that included attention to this transition from the old to the new dispensation. Stated a bit more simply than Schilder put it, his definition goes like this: "Ethics is the science of the constant grounds, the changing dispensations, and the relevant concrete specificity of man's obligation toward God's revealed will" (Schilder 1980, 16). By the phrase "constant grounds," Schilder was referring to those fundamental principles in Scripture that always retain their validity. Man is a creature; in contrast to the animal, man has been brought into a covenant with God; man is the image of God; and the like. By "changing dispensations," Schilder was referring to the transition that occurred between the Old and New Testaments. And the third element of his definition was Schilder's way of indicating that we must also take into account questions like: Where are we living? When are we living? What new questions do technological discoveries and inventions generate? This and much more must be considered in explaining that amid all constancy we find much variety and development in (Christian) morality.

RESPONSIBLE APPEAL TO SCRIPTURE

We should reject the erroneous use of Scripture in ethics that we encounter in, among other things, biblicism. But it is more important that we provide suggestions for a good and proper use of Scripture. Obviously, Scripture can be used in various ways. In certain matters, we can simply appeal to one or more verses, but not in other matters. If I wish to persuade someone that he needs to let go of his anger against a brother, then I can do that with an appeal to Matthew 5:22. But if someone asks me whether Scripture says anything about genetic engineering, everyone understands that appealing to a verse or two here is not helpful. Nevertheless, we do believe that Scripture is a lamp to our feet and a light upon our path for every age and for every moral question. But how?

To answer this, I wish to explain four ways of using the Bible. We will consider using the Bible (1) as a guide, (2) as a guard, (3) as a compass, and (4) as a source of examples.

Scripture as a Guide

When I speak of Scripture as a *guide*, I am saying that in numerous instances using the Bible consists simply of appealing to certain verses that everybody can and must find persuasive. Just as a guide points out our route in mountainous terrain, so too we know from Scripture what it is that we—all of us—must or must not do. The command to love one's neighbor and the prohibition against murdering him, or robbing him, or deceiving him, can, together with many other commands and prohibitions, be supported simply with Bible verses. No matter how difficult it is for us to quit living in anger against a brother (Matt. 5:22), to act cordially toward our opponent (Matt. 5:25), to avoid looking at a woman lustfully (Matt. 5:28), or to love our enemy (Matt. 5:44ff.), the difficulty lies not in the ambiguity of God's (or Christ's) will, but in us. A simple appeal to the Decalogue, citing a piece of wisdom from Proverbs or a word of Jesus from the Sermon on the Mount, hits the target here.

It is good for us to begin with this way of using the Bible. For we would be exaggerating if we were to say that our use of Scripture is always accompanied with challenges. In numerous situations in ordinary life, those challenges simply don't exist. This appears clearly from the fact that often we don't even need to open our Bible to convince ourselves or someone else what God's will is. What we consider to be self-evident, because we have the Ten Commandments or other Bible passages clearly in our mind, is self-evident to others as well. Often Scripture is our guide down pathways that we have traveled since we were young. This is not to say, of course, that we always walk down these pathways.

Scripture as a Guard

Scripture also provides support in situations where an appeal to Bible verses is not possible in the sense we've just discussed. In addition to being our guide, Scripture is also our *guard*. What does this mean? Whereas a guide knows just the right path to take across a certain terrain, a guard is someone who warns. To illustrate the meaning of Scripture as a guard, I first need to discuss the following.

The moral climate of both Old and New Testaments is different from the climate we live in today. Husbands and wives, parents and children, governments and citizens, deal differently with each other than in Bible times. A father used to arrange his daughter's marriage (1 Cor. 7:36ff.), something we would consider strange today. In the Bible, slavery is circumscribed, but not condemned—again, something we would view as evil today. Even good kings like David were not averse to killing prisoners of war (2 Sam. 8:2), whereas we would consider that to be a violation of human rights today. Freedom of religion, or the right to change one's religion, was unimaginable within Israel. Scripture nowhere recommends a democratic republican form of government.

As we consider these and similar examples, we have to say that they involve the *historical* development of customs and practices. We saw earlier that, in connection with the Mosaic legislation, we need to keep in mind the progress of *salvation history*. But we must keep another factor in mind. In addition to the progress of salvation history, there is also progress in "ordinary" history. It is not enough to say, "We live after Christ and we are not Israel." We must add, "We live in this time and therefore we cannot act as though we are still living in the time of the Bible." If we take seriously the development and refinement of judicial legislation, the recognition of human rights, and the pervasiveness of democracy, then for those reasons we cannot desire to return to the civil law of Israel. To do so is not only to try to get back beyond the fulfillment of these laws in Christ, but also to forget that since Christ's life on earth, two thousand years have passed. The developments that have led to a better jurisprudence, to the recognition of human rights, etc., are not extensions of Scripture, which for that matter nowhere call for these changes we've been mentioning. But they are extensions of history, a history whose irresistible power sooner or later makes people aware of glaring contradictions and impels them to reorganize antiquated structures, with or without force. That's how things went with regard to religious persecution, with slavery, with child labor, and with colonialism. Various Christian and non-Christian influences played a role in the process of raising people's awareness preceding these enormous changes in human society. The correctness of various changes we all find, sooner or later, to be so self-evident that it strikes us as strange to meet people who still refuse to accept such changes.

But . . . it is not possible to appeal to Scripture to justify these changes. Isn't Scripture important at this point, then? Yes, it is important, but then as a guard who warns us when God is being despised or people are being oppressed. Scripture is not a manual for political and economic developments.

Neither Moses nor another Old Testament prophet provides us with building blocks for that endeavor. But Scripture nonetheless is significant for politics and economics. After all, the *negative* is also important. Old Testament prophets railed against abuses where God was not being honored and people were not being respected. With Bible in hand, we cannot simply declare that slavery must be abolished. In Bible times, slavery was widespread, even in Israel. But even though Scripture does not always tell us how things should go, not by a long shot, it does always tell us how they should not go. If people are being treated unjustly or even scandalously, we must say no to such abuse. So it was that in the course of history, slavery and apartheid were unmasked as evil, and both were dismantled. Therefore, in the "impingement" brought by such developments, we may indeed see God at work, the God who restrains evil in this world and uses people, unbelievers as well as believers, to develop better structures. For we know God not only from the special revelation in Holy Scripture, but also as He has revealed Himself in creation and in world history (Belgic Confession, art. 2).

From this consideration, we conclude that for forming our ethical judgment, it is not enough in many situations simply to be familiar with the Scriptures. We must also know history, which is governed by the same God whom we come to know in Scripture.

By formulating it this way, I have also provided a reply to one objection that people might make. Someone might wonder when in fact certain developments do impinge upon us with irresistible force and when we may in fact see God's hand in them. Are there not also matters that many people find self-evident that are in fact *not* morally good? Here is an example: In the years before World War II, did not some German Christians insist that it was God's will that Hitler become the leader of the German nation? Was not Hitler the man whose arrival occurred with irresistible force as a gift from God? Of course, these German Christians appealed to God's general revelation, but they refused to see that Hitler's ideology of national socialism and his persecution of the Jews clearly conflicted with Holy Scripture. They closed their eyes to the evil, whereas Scripture exposes such evil. The tree is known by its fruit, and for that reason everyone in Germany at that time could, with Scripture in hand, have exposed Hitler as an enemy of God. Once more, Scripture doesn't always tell us what is morally right for this day and age, but it does show us what in this day and age is evil. Anyone who truly sees this is using Scripture as a guard.

Scripture as a Compass

In some situations, Scripture serves not so much as a guide or guard, but rather as a compass. It provides orientation. Rather than functioning as a guide to tell us concretely what is good or bad, Scripture functions as a compass to point out the direction we should move to find our answer to the question of what is good or bad in a given situation. Consider, for example, the new problems arising in connection with the discovery of DNA or the development of in-vitro fertilization. Some argue that Christian ethics provides no answers in these matters. That would be ridiculous, since we will always face questions in the biomedical sector. Would we then derive nothing from Scripture at that point?

Of course it is true that Scripture nowhere says anything directly about DNA, in-vitro fertilization, etc. An ethics for

DNA experiments can exist only after DNA has been discovered. But even though there is no particular Bible verse dealing with developments in DNA research, the Bible does contain general *themes* that are relevant to the most modern developments. Themes like respect for every human life, for marriage as a monogamous institution, for man being created with a "unique nature"—all of these are relevant today as we reflect on in-vitro fertilization and genetic engineering.

We are dealing here with those constant factors that continue in force throughout every generation and remain applicable to the most advanced scientific developments. We continually wonder, with the assistance of Scripture as our compass, whether it is in accord with the will of God, who has ordained us to be rulers and not creators, for us to proceed further in this or that direction with our research and its applications.

Scripture Points to Examples

The preceding is adequate reason to maintain the claim that Scripture sheds light on modern ethical questions as well. We do not always use Scripture in the same manner. It can function as a guide, a guard, or a compass. But there is one more way it can be used. Scripture contains examples that we are called to follow. We must walk in the footsteps of the saints who lived during the times of the Old and New Testaments, and we must follow them (Luke 4:25ff.; 1 Cor. 10:1ff.; Phil. 3:17; 2 Thess. 3:9; Heb. 6:12; 11:1–12:1ff.; James 5:17–18). The great example, of course, is Jesus Christ Himself (Matt. 16:24; 19:21; John 13:15; 1 Cor. 11:1; 1 Peter 2:21).

Were we to use Scripture only according to the functions explained earlier, as a guide, a guard, and a compass, we would do a serious injustice to the Bible. For Scripture is more than a book from which we draw verses that function to defend or rule out certain actions. It is the book of the covenant between God and humanity, and it provides us with the history of God's redemption of people through Christ. The Bible holds before us how we by faith come to belong to the church of God and Christ. Within this fellowship of faith, the Christian ethos is born. As the story is told to us of Christ and of all who have followed Him, then we are moved to faith and action. "But you have not so learned Christ" (Eph. 4:20).

The importance of Scripture's examples appears from the fact that the apostles do more than repeat "what is written." In cases where a simple appeal to the Decalogue, for example, would have been apparent, they point us to living "in Christ." Or both can be done simultaneously. In Ephesians 6:2–3, Paul mentions the fifth commandment, but he does not start with that precept. The first thing he says is, "Children, obey your parents *in the Lord* [Jesus]" (Eph. 6:1). As in numerous other instances, the motive here is following Christ. Christians must walk differently than pagans, not (only) because the Ten Commandments require that, but because they have learned to know Christ (Eph. 4:20). They must be forgiving toward others, even as God has bestowed forgiveness upon them in Christ (Eph. 4:32). They must test what is acceptable to the Lord (Eph. 5:10). In their marriages, husbands and wives must reflect the relationship between Christ and His church (Eph. 5:22ff.). Christians must avoid sexual impurity, because their bodies are members of Christ (1 Cor. 6:3ff.). These are only a few of many similar exhortations.

Therefore, we can even say that Scripture is used as a guide, a guard, and a compass only by one who stands in a living relationship with Christ and His church. The example of Christ and His followers summons us to be closely bound to the church as His body, in order to inquire both within and along with that fellowship concerning the will of God. That is very important for our reflection on the Christian lifestyle, among other things.

A simple and direct appeal to Bible verses is not always possible. What must the pastor say to his catechism students about dancing, barhopping, movies, and television? He cannot simply come with a bunch of Bible verses. But whether the issue is sports, card playing, alcohol, smoking, movies, television, or something else, the decision involves a person's lifestyle and various concrete features of that style—a decision, then, that constitutes an answer to the question, Who am I, as I live before the face of Christ? Who may and must I be?

USING OUR UNDERSTANDING

So we can use Scripture in various ways. At the same time, it has also become evident that we need more than Scripture. We obtain our knowledge of issues from more than just Scripture alone. Anyone reflecting on an issue like a medical or a political problem must possess knowledge of medical or political affairs. Naturally, we do not obtain that kind of knowledge from the Bible. Although the Bible is indispensable for Christian ethics, it is not the only source of our knowledge.

What John Calvin wrote about our understanding is helpful at this point. He distinguished between the *ratio ingenita*, which everybody has by nature; the *ratio vitiosa*, resulting from human depravity; and the *tertia ratio*, which is directed by God and His Word (1863–1900, 9:474).

The *ratio ingenita* (literally, "the understanding we have received at our birth") can lead humanity to good insights and good actions in various matters, even apart from any knowledge of the Scriptures. How could Calvin and others say something like this?

They believed in divine providence, whereby God distributes gifts of understanding among people. Those gifts are surely not bestowed only upon Christians. Also to non-Christians does God give insight into various matters. For that reason, we can often reach mutually agreeable conclusions by using our "common sense." The *ratio vitiosa* (literally, "the erroneous understanding, which does not function properly due to our sin") is the cause of people, including we ourselves, doing many things completely wrongly. At that point, we are *not* using our understanding well.

Fortunately, there is still the *tertia ratio* (literally, "the third understanding"), whereby we proceed in a proper way, led by the light of Scripture. If we use these distinctions, then we might say that the *tertia ratio* equips us to use Scripture as a guard and a compass. We employ "ordinary" knowledge of things that we need for our ethical reflection, but at the same time we are led by what Scripture has to say about the issue at hand.

So in every issue we must use our ordinary understanding. The Reformers appealed confidently not only to Scripture, but also to nature or to reason in order to establish the evidence for particular decisions. Calvin, for example, mentions in the *Institutes* that every nation has the liberty to make laws that seem profitable to them. The only condition is that everywhere the principle of love must serve as the foundation (4.20.15).

It is interesting to notice what Calvin writes next. In all of our laws, writes Calvin, we must attend to two things: the *precept* (*constitutio*) of the law and the *equity* (*aequitas*) of the law. Precepts may indeed vary, as long as they are directed toward the single aim of equity. Such equity is the goal, rule, and limit of every law. Laws must be characterized by humaneness (*humanitas*). They must fit the situation of time, place, and people. Calvin dared to say even that occasionally other laws do that better than the law of Moses (*Institutes* 4.20.15–16)!

Such observations are important for those involved in legal and political issues, but are just as important for our ethical reflection. For we must inquire not only concerning the letter of the (biblical) law, but also concerning the spirit of the law. What Jesus said about the Sabbath can be said of all the commandments: "The Sabbath was made for man, and not man for the Sabbath" (Mark 2:27). To apply divine precepts in such a way as to force human life into a straitjacket is surely to trod the wrong path.

If we understand what equity is, then we will be on guard against a biblicistic use of Scripture and an insistence upon antiquated ethical opinions. The route for renewed reflection must always remain open. We need not try to avoid developments that confront us with new questions. The abiding command of God, given to us clearly in Scripture, we must obey in our circumstances and in our day. For that, we need not only Scripture, but understanding as well. We need understanding, not in the sense of autonomous reason, whereby a person can make out what is good and what is bad apart from God, but in the sense of Psalm 119:34: "Give me understanding, and I shall keep Your law; indeed, I shall observe it with my whole heart."

BE CAREFUL FOR MOTIFS

Everything can be abused. Even the notion of equity. People can play this off against the existing order. An appeal to the "spirit" of the law can leave no room for the "letter" of the law.

We can see this more clearly if we recall the word used a moment ago in connection with equity: the word *humaneness*. In contemporary ethics that has no room for God, humaneness easily becomes the dominant theme. Everything must be directed according to what is humane, what makes for human dignity.

Now, we too consider the notion of humaneness extremely valuable. But what is the content of this notion? Is this notion given a biblical content, or does modern man himself determine what must be considered humane or inhumane? Let me illustrate. If things are not going so smoothly in a marriage, and one or both of the partners can find solace and satisfaction with a third party, can we say that this solution serves the cultivation of humaneness? A person who considers humaneness a central ethical theme *and therefore supplies it with his own content* will probably answer affirmatively. But a Christian knows the saying of Jesus, that anyone who looks at a woman lustfully has already committed adultery with her in his heart (Matt. 5:28). He knows from various Scripture passages that marriage is a holy institution that may not be violated. He believes that the seventh commandment is good and wholesome for a person, and for that reason he could never consider marital unfaithfulness as humane. Perhaps such a solution looks entirely humane, but it is not humane for someone for whom Scripture prescribes what is genuinely humane.

Earlier in this chapter we saw how dangerous it is to appeal to isolated verses. But it is just as dangerous to appeal to a motif or a theme while closing our eyes to Bible verses. That applies to motifs like humaneness and so many others that function in ethics, like justice, happiness, and love. Such motifs are wholly biblical and Christian, as long as they receive their biblical and Christian content.

That is especially true of love, concerning which Scripture says that it does one's neighbor no evil (Rom. 13:10). Suppose for a moment that two lovers engage in premarital sex, or two people live in a homosexual relationship. They are apparently convinced that neither party is injuring the other, and that in fact they are showing love toward each other. Does their conduct constitute the kind of love that God requires of us? Can we simply posit this rule: Love and do what you want? On the contrary, in this way love is being played off against the Bible. God has not only given us the command to love, but also identified that which love must pursue. The question becomes, Do premarital sex and homosexual conduct satisfy that requirement of love, or do these behaviors contradict every form of love that God desires?

Occasionally, theological themes can function prominently in ethics as well. Think of the familiar triad of creation, reconciliation, and redemption. Each of these three can be emphasized so one-sidedly that the fullness of biblical revelation is violated.

In emphasizing the theme of *creation*, one can speak of creation ordinances in such a way as to absolutize them. This leads to viewing existing social and political relationships as though they were creation ordinances, when in fact they are frequently nothing but cultural forms that have had their day.

The doctrine of creation ordinances has been quite influential, especially in Lutheran ethics. The danger of conservatism, an attitude of being unwilling to be open to new relationships, is not imaginary. We need to pay attention to creation ordinances. Recall what Genesis 1–2 says about human dominion over creation, about labor and marriage. But we must always factor in the significance for such creation ordinances of redemption through Christ as well.

In emphasizing the motif of *reconciliation*, one could indeed argue that it has actually already happened: at Golgotha. Christ has purchased us, and we have been liberated from slavery and death. Nevertheless, here too the wrong thing can be emphasized, leading to a pietistic malformation of our conduct. Christ's work of reconciliation cannot be conceived of apart from its relationship to creation and to re-creation. Ethics must not become an individualistic enterprise, but must also pursue what is wholesome for the world. Ethics is interested not simply in the conversion of the person, but also in social and political issues.

In emphasizing the theme of *redemption*, one runs the risk of focusing all his attention on the new and the novel. Does not Scripture tell us that all things will be made new (Rev. 21:5)? Driven by such an eschatological motif, people easily dispense with the old. The established order must disappear; existing economic, social, and political structures must be dismantled. *Revolution* and *liberation* are key words. In modern ethics, this eschatological motif received much attention from 1970 to 1990, when many theologians allowed themselves to be seduced by Marxist notions of world improvement. People lost sight of the reconciliation that Christ had accomplished. There is no peace for anybody, if peace and justice do not govern the world of politics. Everything had to be overturned. Naturally, any talk of creation ordinances was from the devil.

Be careful for the one-sided application of motifs! Those themes in themselves are fine, and everybody uses them. But we must always try to let the whole Scripture resonate in our ethics. So we avoid every form of biblicism that seeks to tie our decisions to isolated verses. But we also avoid every theme or motif that is isolated from Bible verses to live a life of its own.

MATURITY AND DISCERNMENT

As we come to the end of this chapter, it may seem that using Scripture is a difficult enterprise for Christian ethics. Indeed, we don't have answers to various ethical questions within easy grasp, no matter how firmly convinced we may be that God's Word is a lamp for our feet and a light upon our path.

Nevertheless, we should look at those difficulties in another way. The reality that we need to reflect upon many issues we face, without having ready answers to many of our questions, is no shame but rather an honor. Whereas during the Old Testament dispensation Israel was led by the hand and kept immature, something else characterizes the New Testament church. Her glory consists in her maturity (Gal. 4:1ff.). We no longer live on milk, as infants do, but on solid food, as adults. Through experience and practice, our senses are sharpened to distinguish between good and evil (Heb. 5:12ff.). We may seek to discover what is pleasing to the Lord (Eph. 5:10). Paul prays that the love of the Philippians may continue to abound more and more "in knowledge and all discernment, that you may approve the things that are excellent" (Phil. 1:9–10).

Illuminated by the Holy Spirit, we will be equipped to use Scripture in a valid manner. We will surely encounter difficulties in learning to distinguish what is excellent, though we must not overemphasize them.

In fact, we do not have to solve the problems that arise all by ourselves. We live within the fellowship of the church, which includes generations of believers who, before we were born, also listened to the Scriptures and left behind their answers. Today as well, we don't stand alone. We must engage in our ethical reflection together with others who face the same issues and with us desire to listen to Scripture.

To say that each person must determine between himself and God what he should do and not do is individualistic. The Holy Spirit binds us to one another and desires that we be considerate of each other, even when our insights differ (Rom. 14–15; 1 Cor. 8–11). If we need to travel our own way, then we must know why. "Let each [person] be fully convinced in his own mind" (Rom. 14:5). That is a powerful summons! Each person must know what he is doing. His action must proceed from his inwardly firm conviction. That is quite different from the attitude of live and let live. In the church of Christ, we are not grains of sand, but members of the same body. In our maturity, we must be willing to explain our viewpoint. Maturity is something different from individualism.

The Bible passages we are referring to lead us into a completely different sphere from that of uniform legalism ("We must all think and act alike") or that of rigid moral custom ("It was good enough for our forefathers, so it can stay that way today"). We must keep on praying for clear insight and sensitivity. To pray for a renewed mind is to pray for the ability to discern God's will, His good and acceptable and perfect will (Rom. 12:2). Thereby we are shown not necessarily the easiest, but surely the best, path to walk. Bound to Scripture and led by the Spirit, we make our decisions in the liberty to which Christ has called us, that we may live as sons and not as slaves (Gal. 5:1ff.).

Literature

Calvin, John. 1863–1900. *Ioannis Calvini opera quae supersunt omnia.* Edited by Guilielmus Baum, Eduardus Cunitz, and Eduardus Reuss. Brunsvigae: C. A. Schwetschke.

Loonstra, B. 1994. *De geloofwaardigheid van de Bijbel.* Zoetermeer: Boekencentrum.

Perkins, William. 1642. *The whole treatise of the cases of conscience.* London: John Legatt.

Schilder, Klaas. 1980. *Dictaten kompendium der ethiek I–IV.* Collected by G. J. Bruijn. Kampen: Van den Berg.

Wierenga, L. 1996. *De macht van de taal en de taal van de macht.* Kampen: Kok-Voorhoeve.

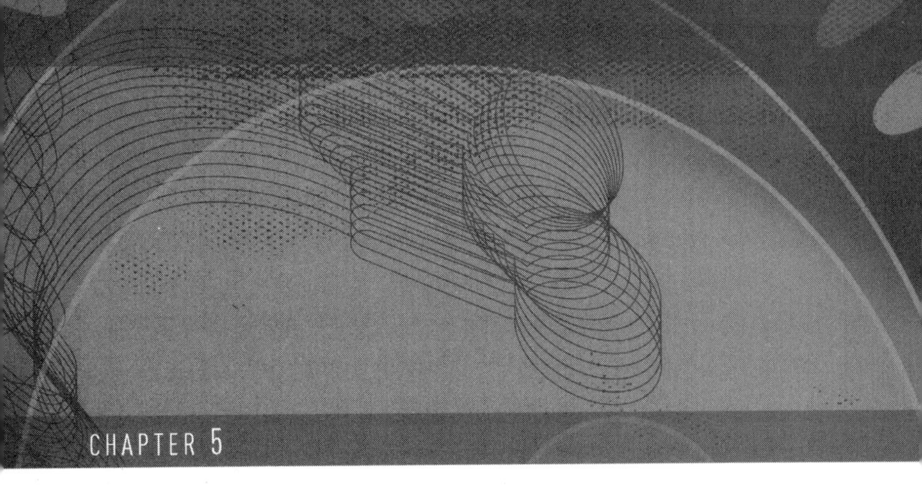

The Ten Commandments

CORE COMMANDMENTS

As we reflect on responsible conduct in a Christian way, we might be wondering what portion of Scripture receives the most discussion. The answer: the Ten Commandments. We may assume that already in Israel the Decalogue (literally, "the ten words") constituted a fixed body of instruction for the youth. It was certainly so in the church. Long before the time of the Reformation, the church's instruction was concentrated on the Ten Commandments, the Apostles' Creed, and the Lord's Prayer. We find those core items in the catechisms of the Reformers. In Luther's Large and Small Catechism (1529), the explanation of the Decalogue precedes the discussion of the Apostles' Creed and the Lord's Prayer. In his Genevan Catechism, Calvin treats first the Apostles' Creed, then the Decalogue, and finally the Lord's Prayer. Especially Calvin found the Decalogue to be the expression of God's will for the believer's life. Reformed theology has followed his lead here. One could confidently say that the Heidelberg Catechism and the Westminster Larger and Shorter Catechisms, with their explanations of the Decalogue, have for centuries constituted the backbone of moral instruction in Reformed churches. The Heidelberg Catechism (1563) devotes no fewer than ten of the fifty-two Lord's Days to the Ten Commandments.

In the preceding chapter, I explained among other things that in Christian ethics we are dealing with the whole Scripture. So we cannot possibly restrict ourselves to the Ten Commandments. Many other portions of Scripture come into view when we deal with Christian ethics. Think of the Sermon on the Mount in Matthew 5–7, or the song of love in 1 Corinthians 13. Nevertheless, in this introduction to Christian ethics, I will be discussing only the Ten Commandments, because we may rightly say that in the Decalogue we are dealing with God's core commandments. I will show not only that the Decalogue was important for ancient Israel, but also that the New Testament church derives her norm for Christian living from the Decalogue.

First, consider a number of aspects of the Decalogue from Scripture itself. The text of the Ten Commandments (the Decalogue) was given twice, in Exodus 20 and in Deuteronomy 5. Both times the text forms the beginning of the legislation given to Israel. These "words of the covenant" were ceremonially proclaimed in the hearing of Israel as a kind of constitution. They were engraved separately on two stone tablets, "written with the finger of God" (Ex. 31:18), and they were placed in the ark of the covenant (Deut. 10:1–5).

Both the Old and New Testaments show familiarity with the Ten Commandments. Think of Jeremiah 7:9–10, where God says to His people, "Will you steal, murder, commit adultery, swear falsely, burn incense to Baal, and walk after other gods whom you do not know, and then come and stand before Me in this house which is called by My name, and say, 'We are delivered to do all these abominations'?" Hosea 4:2 summarizes with this list: "By swearing and lying, killing and stealing and committing adultery, they break all restraint, with bloodshed after bloodshed." The Decalogue, along with the Shema (Deut. 6:4–9; 11:13–21; Num. 15:37–41), was read daily in the temple and later in the synagogue.

In the New Testament, Jesus tells the rich young man that he must "keep the commandments." To the question of the young man as to which commandments, Jesus replies, "'You shall not murder,' 'You shall not commit adultery,' 'You shall not steal,' 'You shall not bear false witness,' 'Honor your father and your mother'" (Matt. 19:17–19). Here the fifth through the ninth commandments are listed, nearly in the order of the Decalogue.

Paul provides a somewhat similar summary, one that relates to the Decalogue, in Romans 13:9, where he says, "For the commandments, 'You shall not commit adultery,' 'You shall not murder,' 'You shall not steal,' 'You shall not bear false witness,' 'You shall not covet,' and if there is any other commandment, are all summed up in this saying, namely, 'You shall love your neighbor as yourself.'" Here we encounter the sixth through the tenth commandments.

James 2:11 lists the sixth and seventh commandments: "For He who said, 'Do not commit adultery,' also said, 'Do not murder.'" The Decalogue also clearly influenced the order of the list of vices that we find in 1 Timothy 1:9–10: "The law is not made for a righteous person, but for the lawless and insubordinate, for the ungodly and for sinners, for the unholy and profane [recall the first table of the Decalogue!], for murderers of fathers and murderers of mothers, for manslayers, for fornicators, for sodomites, for kidnappers, for liars, for perjurers, and if there is any other thing that is contrary to sound doctrine . . ." Here is reflected the order of the second table, from the fifth commandment forbidding the murdering of fathers (or, with a view to Ex. 21:15, probably better rendered, "those who strike their father and mother"), to the ninth commandment condemning liars. The eighth commandment prohibits kidnapping. This was an important aspect of this commandment in former times (see Ex. 21:16). Slave traders, extortionists, and pimps are in violation of this commandment! Even today this aspect of the eighth commandment is quite relevant. You need only to think of hostages being taken aboard airplanes, where captors are in fact the masters of others!

These references are adequate to show that the Decalogue occupies a unique place in Scripture. Someone has properly spoken of "the Torah within the Torah" (Van den Berg 1963). The Torah (legislation) of Moses consists of hundreds of regulations, but within that Torah we find another Torah, consisting of the core commandments that are just as familiar to us as they were to the ancient Israelites.

IS THE CHURCH STILL AT SINAI?

But everyone does not accept the view that the Ten Commandments occupy a key position in Scripture. Often it is objected that the Decalogue originated in the Old Testament. How can we who live after Christ's resurrection still seek the core commands for Christian living in the Decalogue? Hugo

Röthlisberger has written a book about this, entitled *Kirche am Sinai* (The Church at Sinai). A church that places the Ten Commandments so centrally in her teaching ministry has, according to Röthlisberger, become stuck at Sinai and cannot be called a New Testament church. Let's look a bit more closely at his arguments, for a lot depends on this point.

Röthlisberger believes that in New Testament "catechesis" the Ten Commandments played no role whatever. Various other elements played a role, according to him, like the motif of light and darkness, the motif of love and that of following Christ. But nowhere has the Decalogue been the starting point for moral instruction. According to Röthlisberger, it could not, because Christ is called the end of the law (Rom. 10:4). The church cannot remain at Sinai, because the old covenant has passed away. Christ has appeared in place of the law. One who is united to Him and lives out of love has fulfilled the law. Whatever God demands of us, He provides to us as fruit of the Spirit. We must examine the will of God. The concrete meaning of love and following Christ must be examined over and over again. In any case, the church is not told in Sinai-fashion (the Ten Commandments!) what God expects of her.

So, is there then no longer a central place for the Decalogue? There is a central place for the motif of love; does it automatically point the way for us, without our being bound by the Decalogue? When we look more carefully at how Röthlisberger defends his view on the absence of the Decalogue in the moral teaching of the New Testament, we are struck by something strange. He can maintain his view only by cutting Scripture apart. For example, in Ephesians 6:2 Paul commands children to obey their parents, appealing to the fifth commandment: "Honor your father and your mother." That contradicts Röthlisberger's opinion. But Röthlisberger thinks that Ephesians 6:2 is a later insertion and does not come from Paul himself! Regarding the gospel of Matthew, Röthlisberger says that the passages that refer to Sinai and the Decalogue (see, for example, Matt. 5:17–20 and 19:18–19) leave us in the lurch in answering the question of the extent to which Christians are under Jewish law or are free from it. Moreover, James 2:11, which quotes the sixth and seventh commandments, as we saw, has no authority for Röthlisberger. In his view, the epistle of James reflects a later development that must be seen as a return to Judaism (Röthlisberger 1965, 13–36, 130, 145).

THE LAW: NOT A WAY OF SALVATION, BUT A NORM FOR LIVING

We need to discuss this matter a bit more. Röthlisberger may dismiss those New Testament passages that don't fit his case, but is he right in appealing to Romans 10:4? Does that verse clearly say that Christ is the end of the law? Does that apply to the law of the Ten Commandments?

In a certain sense, that is correct. When Paul says that Christ is the end of the law, he means that the law *as a way of salvation* has passed away. We are no longer under the law, but under grace (Rom. 6:14). Through Christ, we have died to the law (Rom. 7:1, 4). We have died to the law in order to live to God (Gal. 2:19). The law was a tutor unto Christ, so that we might be justified by faith (Gal. 3:24). This rejection of the law as a way of salvation applies to the entire law in all its facets. So it is not the case that Christ is indeed the end of the law in terms of its ceremonial requirements and not in terms of its moral demands. The rejection of the works of the law as a way of salvation applies to all human works and accomplishments—not only when it comes to obeying the Ten Commandments, but also when it comes to doing good works as the fruit of love. Love, as the "new commandment" (John 13:14), cannot justify us before God any more than fulfilling any other commandment.

But even when we fully recognize this truth, we still cannot say that "the end of the law" means that the Decalogue can be ignored. The very same Paul who said that Christ is the end of the law also said clearly that the law is holy and that the commandment is holy, just, and good (Rom. 7:12, 14). We are indeed free from the yoke and the curse of the law, but that doesn't mean that we are free from the commandments and norms of the law. When the New Testament talks about our freedom from the law, that does not entail an alteration in the validity of the law, but rather a change in the position of the believer who has been liberated by Christ from the curse of the law. The requirement of the law remains, but it is now fulfilled in us who walk not according to the flesh, but according to the Spirit (Rom. 8:4). The law remains the same, but we have changed—in Christ!

It is very important that we understand the connection between *law and liberty*. We are liberated from the curse and the yoke of the law. But that does not mean that the law itself is a curse and a yoke. Romans 7:7–12 is instructive on this point. "Is the law sin?" Paul asks. He answers, "Certainly not! On the contrary, I would not have known sin except through the law. For I would not have known covetousness unless the law had said, 'You shall not covet' " (Rom. 7:7). Genuine misery is located not in the law, but in the human heart: "But sin, taking opportunity by the commandment, produced in me all manner of evil desire. For apart from the law sin was dead. I was alive once without the law, but when the commandment came, sin revived and I died. And the commandment, *which was to bring life*, I found to bring death. For *sin*, taking occasion by the commandment, deceived me, and by it killed me" (Rom. 7:8–11).

The commandment, which itself is holy, righteous, and good, became deadly, because the evil human heart resists it. It is even the case that this good law awakened the slumbering sin! As soon as the commandment said, "You shall not covet," I began longing for just the thing forbidden. So the commandment activates the evil in me, and in that manner the law, which was supposed to lead to life, becomes for me a stimulus unto death. But anyone who is a new creature in Christ (2 Cor. 5:17) enjoys a new relationship to the law.

Or, to say it better, the believer has a renewed relationship to the law. For the original intention of the law comes again to light. Anyone who plumbs the depth of the law understands it, with James, as the law of liberty (James 1:25). He sees the law once again as the law of the living God who saves us. It does not constitute a regimen of sweat and stripes for slaves, but life-rules for the free children of God. This is how the Ten Commandments are understood in the correct way. What water is for fish and air for birds (namely, their life element), such is the law for the children of God.

The Ten Commandments cannot be interpreted well if we ignore the way they are introduced. Pay attention to the *preamble*, which goes like this: "I am the LORD your God, who brought you out of the land of Egypt, out of the house of bondage" (Ex. 20:2; Deut. 5:6). *First* redemption is mentioned, and *then* come the Ten Commandments. From this, the purpose of the Ten Commandments becomes clear. They are given by God to His people in order to *keep* them free. Just as the great redemptive event of the Old Testament (the exodus from Egypt) introduced the commandments, so too the great redemptive event of the New Testament (Christ's resurrection) precedes our life of gratitude. The curse of the law has been removed. That rescue is established in Christ, without our having to lift one finger to keep the law of the Ten Commandments or any other law. But even so, Christ has not come to abolish the law (including the law of the Ten Commandments), but to fulfill it (Matt. 5:17). The song we know as Psalm 119 can be sung also in the Christian church in praise of the law.

THE DEPTH OF THE COMMANDMENTS

So the church should definitely not stay standing at Sinai. Her ethics would degenerate into moralism and legalism if she never understood Christian ethics. That word "Christian" means that we proceed from Christ's work, even though through Him we come back to the Ten Commandments. Notice, in this connection, several things.

In the first place, Christ pointed out the depth of God's commandments. He did this especially in the Sermon on the Mount (Matt. 5:17–48). We who have been taught by the Sermon on the Mount cannot escape the reach of the Ten Commandments through a superficial, literalistic interpretation. Christ teaches us that someone who has never committed murder can still be guilty of violating the sixth commandment if he calls a fellow believer "dimwit" or "fool" (Matt. 5:21–22). And someone who merely looks lustfully at a woman thereby transgresses the seventh commandment (Matt. 5:27–28). Christ has wiped the dust off the law and restored its holy luster. He has placed the law in its fullest meaning, squarely before His disciples and before us. Especially the Reformation understood this message, when it interpreted each of the Ten Commandments per synecdoche (that is, as including the whole field of action and attitude identified by the part mentioned in the commandment; the Greek word *sunekdechesthai* means "to receive jointly"). When the commandment declares, "Thou shalt not kill," then it is mentioning but one instance, to which are related an entire constellation of sins. Moreover, we must not settle merely for the negative formulation, but inquire also about the positive requirements. When something is forbidden, what is being commanded? Consequently, the Ten Commandments apparently provide us not with exhaustive descriptions, but with illustrative commands. (You can read more about this in John Calvin's *Institutes of the Christian Religion* 2.8.10.)

In the second place, Christ emphasized the unity of the commandments by pointing us to love as the fulfillment of the law. We may not observe the law (like the Sabbath commandment, for example) in a way that omits mercy (Matt. 12:1–14). The commandments are not legal formulations that we can respect outwardly, while our hearts remain uninvolved. They specifically require the human heart, because human beings are placed in a personal relationship with God and with Christ. God is not looking for a quantitative fulfillment, whereby the law can be dissected into paragraphs and sections; rather, He seeks a qualitative fulfillment in love, where a person devotes to God not his sacrifices, but himself (Matt. 22:37–40; Rom. 13:8–10; 1 Cor. 13; Col. 3:14).

This is another reason why Sinai cannot be isolated from Golgotha. The loving act of God in surrendering Christ to the cross is the presupposition (Rom. 5:8; 8:32–39; Gal. 2:20) and the origin and fountain of our love for God. All human love for God is a response to the love received from God. Love is love of (or from) the Spirit (Rom. 15:30) and fruit of the Spirit (Gal. 5:22). We must love one another, because love is of God. Everyone who loves is born of God (1 John 4:7).

In the third place, every action that is commanded or forbidden in terms of "Moses" obtains a Christocentric character because we are living "in Christ." An excellent example of this is Ephesians 6:2. When Paul tells children that they must obey their parents, he does not suffice with a reference to the fifth commandment. He asks also for obedience "in the Lord" (Christ). Those frequent expressions "in the Lord" and "in Christ" indicate that all of the Christian's life, thought, and action belong to the new creation in Christ (2 Cor. 5:17; Gal. 6:15; Eph. 2:10). Ordinary living in marriage, family, and society is included in living with Christ. Thereby the ordinary is changed and the old (Moses!) becomes new.

This relationship to Christ is so decisive that sufficient arguments can be derived from it alone in order to identify the good and the evil in certain behavior of Christians. An appeal to Old Testament commandments isn't even required to do that. For example, Christians may not be involved in prostitution, because their bodies are members of Christ (1 Cor. 6:13–20). They must put away lying, because as new people in Christ they are members of one another (Eph. 5:25).

This Christocentric character of our conduct helps explain why the church has tied the fourth commandment ("Remember the Sabbath day") to Sunday, the day of Christ's resurrection. The Sabbath was so intertwined with Jewish life under the law that a break at this point was inevitable. The fourth commandment remained in force in the Christian church, along with all the other commandments. Sadly enough, within the church a legalistic stamp has often been placed upon Sabbath observance, something that continues even today among many. A celebration based on the finished work of Christ allows people to rest on Sunday in a way far different from imprisoning Sunday again in a network of regulations. The proper understanding of the fourth commandment is a test case to see whether we have really gone beyond Sinai!

If we interpret the Ten Commandments properly, by relating them to all of Scripture, then we will not succumb to the notion that as the New Testament church we can no longer give the Decalogue a place of honor. It is too simplistic to dismiss the Decalogue with arguments like "We ourselves were never led out of Egypt," or "We no longer observe the Sabbath," or "We don't live in Canaan, enjoying the promise of long life if we obey our parents," or "We would never covet somebody's donkey or oxen." All of this is true, but the conclusion drawn is false. If you want to use these arguments to stop hearing the Decalogue as part of the church's worship, then your argument really advocates shutting the Bible entirely. For no matter what portion of Scripture we read, we are always meeting up with Israelites, Jews, or Gentile Christians with their social circumstances, customs, and problems. But if we proceed on the assumption that the Word given to them is also given to us, then generally speaking we know quite well how to distinguish, in the material found in

Genesis through Revelation, between what applied especially to them and what applies universally to all of us. Even though we have not been brought out of Egypt, we were certainly present when Jesus Christ accomplished the great deliverance from the slavery of sin. And it requires no great leap to move from oxen and donkey to the new car and other desirable things.

If the Decalogue occupies a prominent place in both Old and New Testaments, then we have every confidence in presenting those Ten Commandments to the church today as core commandments. Once more, this requires that the light of the new shine upon the old, the light that has dawned in Christ. But ancient is different from antiquated. The ancient Ten Commandments are not antiquated, but fulfilled. They stand before us in all their fullness, to be read now in the light of the gospel.

THREEFOLD FUNCTION

In vogue already from the time of the Reformation was a distinction that shed clear light on the various functions that the law, especially the Decalogue, has for man. Three aspects, not always mentioned in the same order, appear in the literature under the theme of *usus legis*, or the uses of the law.

1. The *usus legis primus* (first use of the law) involves the significance of the law for public, political life. This is also referred to as the *usus politicus* or *usus civilis*.
2. The *usus legis secundus* (second use of the law) relates to discovering our guilt. Recall the question of the Heidelberg Catechism, "Whence do you know your misery?" The answer: "Out of the law of God." This is

also termed the *usus paedagogicus* or *usus elenchticus*. The reason for this I will explain in a moment.
3. The *usus legis tertius* (third use of the law) points to the significance of the law as a rule of gratitude. This is also called the *usus didacticus* or *usus normativus*.

These distinctions might also be formulated in this way:

1. The law functions as a *barricade*, whereby man is protected against himself.
2. The law functions as a *mirror*, wherein man observes his own miserable situation.
3. The law functions as a *yardstick*, whereby man can shape his gratitude.

With regard to these uses of the law, we could better view them not so much as various uses to which we put the law, but rather as functions that God has assigned to the law. What is *He* doing in our lives with His law? If we always remember this, then we will never isolate one function from the others. They belong together.

The First Function

Let's consider each function in turn. The first function refers to God using the law for maintaining outward discipline and decency. A bridle must be employed, says Calvin, to restrain the dissoluteness of people (*Institutes* 2.7.10). People must be barricaded from evil. The result is important, for only in this way is human society possible. This result does not penetrate very deeply, since only the outside and not the inside of the human heart is affected in this way.

What do the laws by which the government restrains human dissoluteness have to do with the Decalogue? The Reformers made the connection between these quite simply. What had been written in the Decalogue was, according to their conviction, all engraved on the human heart like an innate law, a natural law, or a natural light. Commandments forbidding murder, stealing, adultery, and lying not only would have appeared on the stone tablets of the Ten Commandments, but also would be known "from nature" and would therefore appear in legislation. A verse regularly cited to prove this is Romans 2:14–15, where we are told that pagans do by nature what the law commands and have the work of the law written in their hearts.

It is undoubtedly correct to say that non-Christians have knowledge of things that appear in God's law. Romans 2:14–15 points clearly in this direction. There we read that the work of the law is written in the hearts of (pagan) people. That divine writing has penetrated deeply enough into the hearts of pagans to confront them inescapably with the demands of God's law. But we must keep in mind that Paul is talking about the work of *the* law written in their hearts. In terms of the context of Romans 2, that law is not the natural law, but the law of Moses! Paul does not identify "nature" as the source of the moral norm, of which then the law (the Decalogue) would be a concrete expression; rather, he reasons in precisely the opposite direction. He argues that the power of God's law, as we encounter it in the Scriptures, especially in the Ten Commandments, exerts the kind of divinely applied pressure upon pagans that they do by nature—that is, "of themselves" or "in reality"—what this law of God requires of them.

As long as we understand God to be responsible for the fact that through the ineradicable impression His law makes, order within life and development of life among people are still possible, then we indeed make the proper connection between the average person and his or her knowledge of God's law. However, unfortunately, people occasionally view too highly the knowledge possessed by the natural man. They begin to talk about "innate knowledge" and "natural law," which are supposedly adequate for good conduct and for a good ethics. The *usus politicus* of the law then supposedly teaches us just how much good people are capable of doing. Occasionally this function of the law is declared to be the primary one, as argued by Dutch ethicist G. Th. Rothuizen in his dissertation entitled *Primus usus legis*. In this study, he assigns human capability a place next to and even above Christian ability. According to Rothuizen (1962, 129ff., 216ff.), the world needs to be protected against Christianization. Psalm 8 supposedly puts all things under the feet, not of the believer, but of humanity. In this way, secularization becomes a good thing!

The Reformers certainly did not go in this direction, even when they wrote extensively about innate human knowledge of the law. They did ascribe to man the possession of "natural light," but at the same time acknowledged that man suppresses this light. We can read this in the Augsburg Confession, XVIII, 71–72, and in the Canons of Dort, III/IV, 4. They made no optimistic claims about what man can accomplish without God and without Christ. They never fanned such a small glimmer into a great fire.

But all of this does not take away from the important function served by the *usus primus* of the law. God uses His law to maintain human society, even though people widely abuse God's law and often go no further than an external conformity to that law. We should not isolate the first function from the other two functions. If we do, we will easily endorse natural law, secularization, and the goodness of humanity. And if we go in that direction, then we will soon grant pride of place to human reason. Man saves himself. It is no longer God who uses *His* law to bring order to society, but man himself becomes the norm. Human reason obtains a normative function instead of being a modest instrument or organ in the service of God's will. In his ethics, Helmut Thielicke has correctly pointed out this shift from the *usus organicus* (the organic function) of reason to serve, listen, and obey, to the *usus normativus* (the normative function) of human reason (Thielicke 1979, 143–44).

One final comment on the *usus primus*. If this function is (correctly) tied to the Decalogue, it is improper to limit that function to the second table of the Decalogue. Therefore, we should connect the law's first function not only to horizontal, mutual human relationships, but also to man's vertical relationship to God. One obvious consequence would be that in politics we should not be silent about God!

Sometimes people want to ignore the law's first function. Such is the case in the ethics of N. H. Søe (1957). But if we proceed in this direction, then church and world are no longer clearly distinguished. The outworking of God's law in the world is different from its outworking in the church. A politician deals far more with the "hardness of hearts" than a church leader. Advancing the public order is something different from appealing for conversion of the heart that should happen through the preaching of the law in the church. If you isolate the law's first function, you will fall quickly into humanism. But if you ignore the law's first function and envision the law's outworking only in terms of ecclesiastical style, you will slip into Anabaptism. The Anabaptist closes his eyes to this world with which God in His longsuffering desires to continue working. And if God provides His law to make society for pagans and unbelievers tolerable, then we should not retreat from this world either.

This conclusion is significant for our social ethics. Lending a hand to improve political and social situations is necessary, for example, by eliminating the distressing contrasts between rich and poor countries, or by combating racial discrimination, even though this does not lead to the conversion of the people for whom we take up the cudgels. Whenever our political and social conduct can lead to a better order in the world, then we are entirely in line with God's purpose in the law's first function.

The Second Function

In the second place, God uses the law to expose man's misery to him. This function is often derived from Galatians 3:24: "Therefore the law was our tutor [*paedagogus*] to bring us to Christ, that we might be justified by faith." In ancient times, the *paedagogus* was the (unpopular) fellow who had to keep an underage lad in line. He was not a teacher, but a babysitter. This clarifies why the second function came to be termed the *usus paedagogicus* or *usus elenchticus* (the Greek word *elenchein* means "to convict" [of guilt]). Like a babysitter, the law drums into us that we had better forget our excuses, because we stand guilty before God.

Actually, identifying this use with the term *paedagogicus*

is not quite correct, since Galatians 3:24 says that the law *was* our tutor. In redemptive history, the law's function as a tutor has come to an end. Now that faith has come, we no longer stand under the law as our tutor (Gal. 3:25). Nonetheless, we may certainly continue insisting that, now that we have received the law back again as we stand in a new relationship to Christ, we learn to know our misery by looking in the mirror of this law. However, behind the law we must see the Lawgiver, whose intention with His law is not to threaten us, but to grant us life in Christ. We may not uncouple law and gospel. In the light of the gospel, we behold our own sin and weakness all the better. And for that, the law is also a good mirror.

For Martin Luther and the Lutherans, this second function is the genuine and primary function of the law, though they do recognize the first function and, less conspicuously, the third function. Lutherans emphasize the second use of the law, which results in a rather negative view of the law. Often the law's function is described *dialectically*. This means that the second use really has two functions that seem to contradict each other. The law that in itself can bring only death becomes in God's hand the means to repentance. It puts a person to death, but at the same time this death functions through the law as an instrument in God's hand to lead that person to the point of liberation through the gospel.

Nevertheless, this position involves too much abstraction, in my opinion. As I mentioned earlier, we must not disconnect the law from the Lawgiver, or the law from the gospel. Only in their unity do they expose our misery to us. Whenever people talk about a dialectic, we had better watch out. Often the term *dialectic* is used to mean that things that are essentially exclusive are nonetheless actually united. Applied to the law, this term suggests that the law is an ambiguous entity. The law kills, and that is supposedly its "proper" work. At the same time, the law is also to be regarded positively, because God harnesses the law's negative work in order to make a person alive. And that is God's "proper" work. But in this line of thinking, inadequate place is given to the law's evangelical character. Recall once more the preamble of the Decalogue! The law is not at all designed to kill us, but aims at keeping us within the fence of the redemption that God has accomplished. That is the law's proper work. But in our own wickedness, we react against the good law of God in such a way that it becomes a diving board and a beachhead for sin. Through the law, sin becomes virulent (Rom. 3:20).

Even after the law has lost the tutorial function described in Galatians 3:24, we can still continue speaking of the second function of the law as that of exposing our misery. Otherwise, the Christian life becomes superficial, and respectability, moralism, and legalism soon replace the humble confession that Christ is our life.

The Third Function

Finally, we find in God's law also the standard by which a person can shape his or her gratitude. Calvin calls this function the primary one, because it captures the real goal of the law (*Institutes* 2.7.12). For him, the evangelical significance of the law is central. He does not characterize the law negatively, as Luther often does. Someone has remarked that Calvin spoke of this third use of the law as the primary one in a self-conscious polemic with Luther (W. Elert, mentioned in Berkouwer 1971, 158). Among Lutherans, the law's third function often applies only to man as a sinner. The law is a killing law, with which the

Christian has nothing more to do. Law and gospel are kept strictly separate, as are God's holiness and His grace.

Helmut Thielicke has written an ethics book whose fundamental theme is the contradiction between law and gospel in Luther's sense. In his *Theological Ethics,* he writes impressively about the law. According to him, law and gospel must be strictly separated. He even dares to speak of a conflict within God, between the God who accuses us in His law and the God who is gracious toward us in His gospel. This is the only way, according to Thielicke, that the miracle of God's grace can remain a miracle. Grace loses its miraculous character unless alongside it stands the condemning law (Thielicke 1979, 272ff., 332ff.).

What should we say about this? It is good to *distinguish* (but not *separate*) law and gospel. Thielicke properly criticizes Karl Barth, for whom the law was a form of the gospel. Barth permits the gospel to swallow the law, so that the law loses its independence as an accuser, for instance, at the Last Judgment. In fact, Barth's theology has no room for a law that any longer condemns at all, because all people share in Christ's redemption. In this way, Barth cheapens grace, an accusation leveled against him more than once. But we have reservations about Thielicke's position as well. The contrast is not between God's holiness and His grace, or between law and gospel, but between God's law and His gospel, on the one hand, and rebellious man, on the other hand. Because man turns against God, the law obtains a fierceness, *but that is not its "nature."*

Therefore, the law can possess a third function of giving direction for Christian living. The law gives shape to Christian living. For Thielicke, the law cannot do this, because for him the second function of the law is dominant. In the life of the believer, the law does nothing but expose the misery into which the fall into sin has plunged him. The negative formulations of the Decalogue, says Thielicke, point not to natural law, but to natural lawlessness, expressed in killing, stealing, committing adultery, and so forth. He calls the Decalogue (and the Sermon on the Mount as well) a gauze that serves to keep open the wound of our sinful identity (Thielicke 1979, 95 and elsewhere).

Much depends on our judgment on this issue. Is it really the case that we stay stuck in the negative, so that the law can only keep us immature, or is a positive Christian life possible in which the law functions to shape and lead us?

We will deal more extensively with this question in chapter 6. Does a Christian life have its own style or not? Must we conclude, with Thielicke and many others, that what is "Christian" has no unique content, so that we really cannot speak of a Christian lifestyle or a Christian political or social style? Our answer to such questions involves whether or not the law has a third function.

The answer also has everything to do with our social ethics. We saw that the first function compels us to be involved constructively in the world's political and social structures. But the same is true if we accept the third function. God's law, as the standard for our Christian living, gives shape not only to our personal lives, but also to our social lives. The gospel is the salt of the earth and the light of the world (Matt. 5:13–16). Christ has received all authority in heaven and on earth (Matt. 28:18). He lays claim not only to people, but also to the structures within which they live. Political and social life must be subjected to him. It may well be that as Christians we cannot get very far when we summon politicians, businessmen, and scientists to follow Christ. However, we must be directed not by the prospect of success, but by our faith. If you really believe that all authority has been given to Christ, then you must also believe that congressmen, businessmen, academicians, and artists are in all their labors bound to God's law as the rule of gratitude. Christian politics and Christian scientific investigation may well be scarce commodities in this world, but we continue to believe that the law as we have received it again in Christ is a salutary force for all of society in all its relationships.

Clearly something like this penetrates far more deeply than what we saw with the law's first function. That function involves restraining the dissoluteness of man and maintaining a tolerable society, even without converting people to Christ. Here the law's third function involves the penetration of the gospel in a society that listens to Christ.

Literature

Berkouwer, G. C. 1971. *Sin.* Grand Rapids: Eerdmans.

Douma, J. 1996. *The Ten Commandments: Manual for the Christian life.* Translated by Nelson D. Kloosterman. Phillipsburg, N.J.: P&R Publishing.

Röthlisberger, Hugo. 1965. *Kirche am Sinai: Die Zehn Gebote in der christlichen Unterweisung.* Zurich: Zwingli Verlag.

Rothuizen. G. Th. 1962. *Primus usus legis: Studie over het burgerlijk gebruik van de wet.* Kampen: Kok.

Søe, N. H. 1957. *Christliche Ethik: Ein Lehrbuch.* Munich: Chr. Kaiser Verlag.

Thielicke, Helmut. 1979. *Theological ethics.* Vol. 1, *Foundations.* Edited by William H. Lazareth. Philadelphia: Fortress.

Van den Berg. 1963. *De Thora in de Thora.* Aalten: De Graafschap.

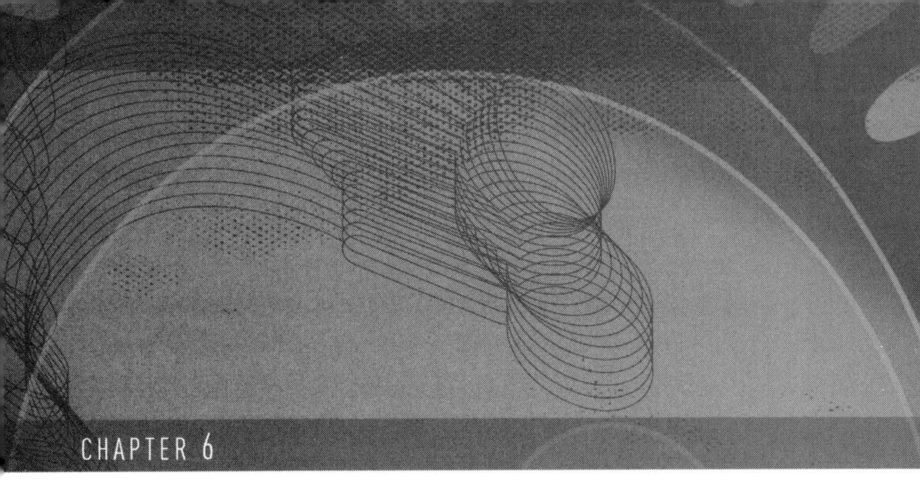

Christian Morality

ONCE MORE: ETHICS AND MORALITY

From the preceding chapters, it is obvious that I indeed wish to speak of a Christian ethics. But can we also say that there is a Christian morality? Just to recall once more the difference: morality is the whole of traditional and prevailing customs, while ethics is reflection upon those customs. If it is admitted that we can reflect upon morality on the basis of a Christian perspective, does that also mean that there is a Christian morality? Do Christians behave so differently in this world from non-Christians that alongside various moralities stands a *Christian* morality? A different behavior is something else than a different reflection. Many today believe that it is entirely meaningless to speak of such a different behavior. Certainly there are different sorts of Christians, and the various behaviors of each sort have something unique about them. But should the Christian faith by definition lead to behavior that is different from that of non-Christians? On the basis of what I have written, especially at the conclusion of chapter 5, it should be clear that I will be answering the question affirmatively. But we need to pause to consider this matter a bit further.

Traditional morality has crumbled to pieces. Christians too have identified with much that has accompanied the new morality. Remarkably, church people have stepped out in front to cast doubt on whether it was so correct in the past to reject the morality of abortion, euthanasia, homosexuality, premarital sex, and the like. In his book *Honest to God*, John A. T. Robinson defended the new morality (1963, chap. 6). Dozens of theologians and ethicists have followed his lead. It is the exception rather than the rule for one of their number to come to the defense of viewpoints cherished in the church until about 1960, viewpoints now surrendered.

For that reason, we are confronted with the question of the uniqueness, or the *proprium* (as the term is used in the field of ethics), of Christian morality. Is there anything unique about it? Or, when you get down to the basics, is there but a single morality for both non-Christians and Christians? Should they not be working together to build one world that honors the same human rights, the same freedom from oppression, and the same experience of what it means to be human? Many theologians are indeed willing to concede that Christians have a unique motivation. Christians act in terms of faith in God. On the basis of that faith, they should be armed against ideologies much better than non-Christians should be. They should have a better understanding of the impermanence of all things. They should know what "eschatology" is and therefore be in a better position to remain open to change. Non-Christians often sense that too, but Christians should know this on the basis of their faith. Therefore, Christians especially should be able to make a critical contribution by explaining how things should not be done and to warn against prejudices taking root and flowering into ideologies that destroy human society. But critical observation is something other than positive defense of a different morality. Is there really a uniquely Christian morality?

WE DO MANY THINGS THE SAME

Let's establish first that in many respects Christians act exactly like non-Christians. When I speak of "Christians," I am referring to people who take their faith seriously and so are not Christians in name only. That we do many things just like our unbelieving neighbors should not surprise us. For in Scripture it is either assumed or stated explicitly that a large part of our behavior is recognizable by the non-Christian. We read that a Christian may not give offense to Jew or Greek (1 Cor. 10:32). He needs to be careful to do what is proper, not only in the eyes of the Lord, but also in the eyes of other people (2 Cor. 8:21). He must conduct himself appropriately toward those who are "outside" (1 Thess. 4:12). He must walk honorably (Rom. 13:13), act decently (1 Cor. 7:35), and not behave rudely (1 Cor. 13:5). Such warnings would be strange, if no obvious agreement were possible between the behavior of Christians and the behavior of non-Christians. How else could Paul have been a Jew to the Jews and a Greek to the Greeks (1 Cor. 9:20)—indeed, pleasing everybody in everything (1 Cor. 10:33)? Such declarations betray the truth that the morality of Christians definitely does not always stand in direct opposition to that of unbelievers. The cross of Christ is an offense to the Jews and a stumbling block to the Greeks

(1 Cor. 1:23), but apparently it is also possible through the Spirit to be a servant of Christ and as such to be acceptable to God *and* approved by men (Rom. 14:18).

The principles of Christian family living, found in Ephesians 6 and Colossians 3, and the Christian virtues summarized in Galatians 5:22 and Colossians 3:12, contain much that surfaces in pagan morality too. The pagan is not so alienated from Christian behavior as to have no appreciation for it. On the contrary, the apostle implies that the behavior of the Christian could impress the pagan because the latter apparently knows what is honorable and decent.

We have already observed that the pagan can have the work of the law written in his heart (Rom. 2:15). Much of what the Decalogue presents to the Christian is quite familiar to the non-Christian. Often he is in a good position to distinguish between good and evil. Something like this is evident in Romans 13, where the government is called an institution of God, called to punish evildoers and to commend those who do good (Rom. 13:3). The government—and how often was not and is not such government a pagan government?—is obviously in a position to distinguish between good and bad. It is quite capable of restraining evil among men.

In everyday life, then, Christians and non-Christians have much of their morality in common. A Christian doesn't live in this world like a crackpot. Even when a Christian holds a special office as a spiritual leader in the church, Paul wants him to be well respected beyond the church as a man of good reputation among outsiders (1 Tim. 3:7).

Apparently, then, the Christian does not live in opposition to the ordinary, universal, and common facets of human living. Friendliness, modesty, moderation, and other virtues are generally recognized. In fact, much of our living involves such ordinariness that we need no Bible verses to know what God's will is.

A DIFFERENT INTERIOR

Still, we would only be touching the surface if we said no more. Let's suppose that every act that a Christian performs is performed also by non-Christians. Even then the full picture of the conduct of the Christian would still look different from that of non-Christians. We could illustrate this with the figure of a magnet. The iron filings, comparable to our distinct actions, are by themselves not very remarkable, but under the force of the magnet they fall into a certain order, comparable to the full picture of our conduct. The context within which the Christian performs his actions varies significantly from that of the non-Christian.

We find a remarkable illustration of that in Titus 2:11–14. In this passage, we are summoned to live soberly, righteously, and piously. We encounter these three notions in pagan literature as well. To put it a bit formally, *sobriety* means that one lives in moderation; *righteousness* means that one gives his neighbor what is due him; and *piety* means that one experiences a direct relationship with God. Here we find a morality in a nutshell, so to speak, with three central words that are familiar also to pagans. Nevertheless, the "Christian" magnet organizes these iron filings in a particular way. Paul seeks a sober, righteous, and pious life on the grounds that God's grace has appeared, bringing salvation to all people, and that we are expecting the appearance of Christ. The life of the Christian flows between the two banks of recalling God's grace and expecting Christ's appearance. Christ is busy purifying a people for Himself, a people zealous for good works (Titus 2:14). Christians are different because they have a different interior. They have learned to know Christ, and thereby their thinking is renewed (Eph. 4:20–24).

We can characterize the new life of the Christian as a life of following Christ. "Following" must not be taken literally. We are not called to live as Christ lived, without fixed address, unmarried, and en route to the cross where He took the sins of the world upon Himself. Following is different than copying. We who follow Christ, as I have explained elsewhere (Douma 1992, 13–19), are characterized by at least three things:

1. We follow Christ by fulfilling the task or calling that He has given us. We follow the Lamb wherever He goes (Rev. 10:4). Even as Christ did what His Father asked of Him, so too we follow Christ. We must man the post that He has assigned to us. That involves our daily work, the daily occupation within which we fulfill our calling, and also our special callings that Christ permits us to fulfill. Christ Himself did not turn away from the difficulties involved in following His Father. He accepted the temptations in the wilderness, faced frequent conflicts with the Pharisees, and traveled the road to the cross. In the same way, we too must accept with patience and perseverance everything connected with our calling.

2. We follow Christ not out of self-interest, but for the sake of God and our neighbor. We seek not ourselves, but the other (1 Cor. 10:32–11:1), and we are ready to forgive him for the evil he does against us (Eph. 4:32). The love that drove Christ is found in us as well (2 Cor. 5:14–15).

3. We follow Christ by accepting suffering, even as He did

not flee tribulation. "If anyone desires to come after Me, let him deny himself, and take up his cross, and follow Me" (Matt. 16:24). That refers to *our* cross and not to the very same cross that Christ bore. We could never bear that cross, and fortunately we need not, but Christ's followers do have the same attitude and readiness to deal with their setbacks in a Christian way. These setbacks include poverty, sickness, and other forms of suffering. They may also include the special form of suffering where we sacrifice enjoyable things for the sake of our faith, or even risk our lives.

A DIFFERENT EXTERIOR

It is impossible that the attitude we possess as followers of Christ does not lead also to lives with a different exterior than the lives of those who don't believe in Christ. The Christian, who has received a new outlook on things, won't be given to doing abnormal things. Things won't look at all strange if he accepts in his life the Decalogue as his rule of gratitude. But behavior that is in fact normal, and which will really cause a life redeemed by Christ to blossom anew, looks quite unusual to our modern world. What ought to be seen as normal is unfortunately viewed as rather strange. Most people maintain a lifestyle that is different from the one held before us in the Decalogue. That is patently obvious every day.

When Paul says that the Christian is "totally different" because he has learned to know Christ, he goes on to show how that "total difference" comes to outward expression. The Christian must quit lying, not let himself be swallowed up by his appetites, no longer steal, not grumble, leave sexual indulgence behind, and flee dirty language and drunkenness

(Eph. 4:25–5:21). Formerly he was darkness, but now he is light through his fellowship with Christ (Eph. 5:8).

Anyone looking carefully at how the world deals with the command of God cannot possibly close his eyes to the reality that alongside a non-Christian morality there is a Christian morality. Perhaps the number of upright Christians is very small, and maybe the majority of Christians have fallen for what can no longer be called "Christian morality." None of that takes away from the mandate—nor, apparently, from the possibility—of a Christian morality: to live without fault or blemish as irreproachable children of God among a devious and degenerate generation, where they shine as illuminating stars (Phil. 2:15).

The scriptural summons to good conduct is unmistakably clear. A wise and understanding person shows by his good conduct that his works are done in wise meekness (James 3:13). The good conduct of Christians among pagans must be so remarkable that upon further reflection they retract their criticisms of Christians (1 Peter 2:12). Women married to unbelieving husbands can by their walk, without words, perhaps win their husbands to the gospel (1 Peter 3:1–2). The good conduct of Christians may well be mocked (and how is that to be explained except that he is not living like the pagans?), but if he continues to live in meekness and fear and with a pure conscience, he can shame his opponents (1 Peter 3:16).

Such passages teach us two things. Deep in their hearts, pagans must acknowledge that Christians are behaving respectably. And secondly, the behavior of Christians is distinct and striking only because people around them want to live their own lives estranged from the service of God. For that reason, Christian living has a character all its own.

From the earliest times, the church has realized this. This is put into words quite well in the *Epistle to Diognetus* (about A.D. 150). Christians differ from other people, we read there, by neither country nor language nor customs. Nowhere do they live in their own cities, nor do they employ a strange language of any kind, nor do they lead a strange life. But, while they live in Greek and non-Greek cities, and while they follow the customs of the land with regard to clothing and food and other matters of daily living, they nonetheless display a wonderful, universally acknowledged, and unique lifestyle. The letter continues:

> They live in their own countries, but only as aliens; they participate in everything as citizens, and endure everything as foreigners. Every foreign country is their fatherland, and every fatherland is foreign. They marry like everyone else, and have children, but they do not expose their offspring. They share their food but not their wives. They are "in the flesh," but they do not live "according to the flesh." They live on earth, but their citizenship is in heaven. They obey the established laws; indeed in their private lives they transcend the laws. They love everyone, and by everyone they are persecuted. They are unknown, yet they are condemned; they are put to death, yet they are brought to life. They are poor, yet they make many rich; they are in need of everything, yet they abound in everything. They are dishonored, yet they are glorified in their dishonor; they are slandered, yet they are vindicated. They are cursed, yet they bless; they are insulted, yet they offer respect. When they do good, they are punished as evildoers; when they are punished, they rejoice as though brought to life. By the Jews

> they are assaulted as foreigners, and by the Greeks they are persecuted, *yet those who hate them are unable to give a reason for their hostility.* (Holmes 1989, 299)

That hits the nail on the head! After all, what is so abnormal about behavior that refuses adultery and licentiousness, conduct that neither aborts nor abandons children? What is so strange about a lifestyle where homosexual behavior is avoided, women enter adulthood with purity, widows and orphans are cared for, strangers find lodging, prisoners receive visits, and the dead are buried with dignity? Time and again these and similar arguments were advanced by writers in the early church to defend their Christian morality as normal morality.

To be sure, this morality is certainly different. But this difference results from a negative attitude toward the command of God, a posture adopted by a deeply sick world. This is why a morality that is entirely normal and human has come to be viewed as something weird and unusual.

CHRISTIAN LIFESTYLE

Nevertheless, there is something to be said for using the phrase *Christian lifestyle* instead of *Christian morality*. By "style" we refer to the entirety of interrelated expressions and forms that serve to characterize a particular artist, school, or movement. One familiar with a particular style recognizes a painter, a sculpture, or even a style of conduct. He might observe that "this is a Rembrandt," or "this is Gothic," or even "this is Christian." It is even possible that the Christian lifestyle contains impure elements, just as a Gothic cathedral can include non-Gothic elements. But as a totality, the entire life or lifestyle can very clearly bear the "Christian" stamp.

The Christian lifestyle involves, as we have seen, following Christ in our own circumstances. Why, then, is it preferable to speak of the Christian lifestyle instead of Christian morality? Because morality always involves what people do in general, even when they happen to be Christians. That is always a corporate or collective enterprise. It involves morality in the form of custom. But customs are always strongly time- and situation-conditioned. Therefore, it is impossible to prescribe a Christian style of conduct for all Christians. A simple example can illustrate this. In a significant number of Christian communions, drinking alcohol is strictly forbidden. There we see the custom (morality) of abstaining from strong drink. But should that be prescribed as the Christian custom for all Christians? No, since even though abstinence is a good custom, we cannot impose this rule on all Christians as the law of God. Where that happens, Christian freedom is injured. An imposed Christian morality always goes hand in hand with legalism. So we should not go in that direction. Within Christian morality, significant variety is possible. On that basis, we may assert that a *single* Christian morality does not exist.

In addition, we know that morality, as observable behavior, does not tell us very much about a person's inner disposition. Imagine all the people who live in a Christian town going to church twice every Sunday. Does that mean that each resident does so out of deep conviction? Or has this simply become a custom, one that people hesitate to violate because they would then be looked down upon by their neighbors? Whoever lives in this town belongs in church twice a Sunday! Another example: Suppose that in this small community there are no dances. In such a situation, a young lady would hardly be tempted to go dancing. But then, for that young lady, whether or not to go dancing is not a genuine Christian decision. But suppose that same young lady doesn't get along so well with her mother, but nevertheless in that situation shows the meaning of self-denial by respecting her mother. In that regard, her behavior proceeds from the inside to the outside! For her, not dancing is merely an outward matter, but obeying her mother signifies following Christ.

What is it, then, that unites upright Christians? Not so much a common morality as a common lifestyle that is not limited to the external, but proceeds from the inside outward, along with the three characteristics we mentioned above. Christian forms (customs, morality) can differ widely, but the Christian lifestyle is the same.

To prevent misunderstanding, let me clarify that when I claim that custom and morality are surface behavior, I am not thereby criticizing Christian custom or morality. We recognize such custom in faithful church attendance, in praying and giving thanks before and after eating, in language usage where swearing is taboo, and the like. I am saying only that people who adhere to a good custom are not thereby necessarily displaying the Christian lifestyle that consists in following Christ. Recall the Pharisees who with their customs accomplished much good. Jesus Himself said, "Therefore whatever they tell you to observe, that observe and do" (Matt. 23:3). But at the same time He criticized the Pharisees for being like whitewashed tombs: outwardly beautiful, but inside full of dead men's bones and all uncleanness (Matt. 23:27).

Elsewhere I have written more extensively about this issue. No matter how good a Christian custom may be, I wrote, it often says nothing about making a choice for Christ and the lifestyle flowing from that choice. Were I to say that displaying Christian love is a Christian *custom*, people would look strangely at me. If only it were true that among Christians it was customary to love one another, to be the least of all, to live without worry, and to be averse to the desires of the flesh! But practical reality teaches us something different. Such things do not become customary on earth, because they are fruits of a struggle, won through God's grace, of the new man against the old. Happily, something that will never become customary in society does come to expression in the lives of many upright Christians who are genuinely serious about what the Christian style of living really is (see Douma 1992, 78–105).

Literature

Holmes, Michael W., ed. 1989. *The apostolic fathers*. Translated by J. B. Lightfoot and J. R. Harmer. 2d ed. Grand Rapids: Baker.

Douma, J. 1992. *Christelijke levensstijl*. Kampen: Van den Berg.

Robinson, John A. T. 1963. *Honest to God*. London: SCM Press.

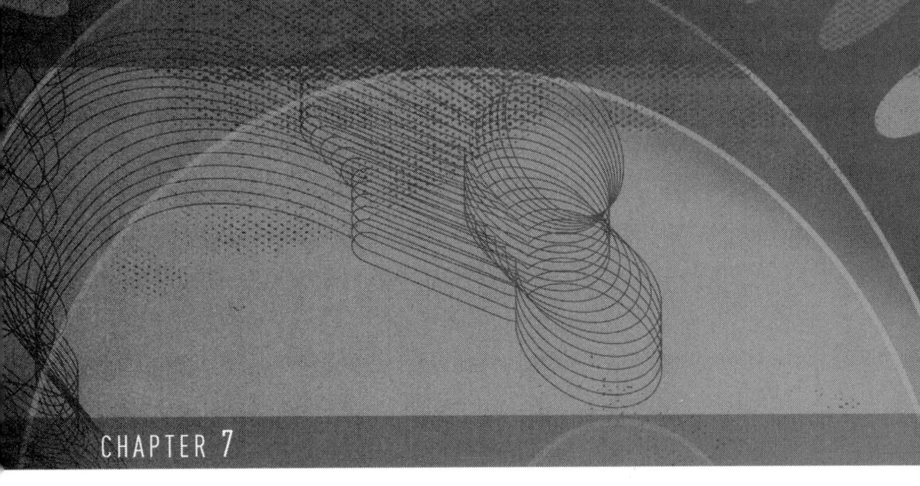

Love

LOVE AND SITUATION ETHICS

If one word should stand at the center of Christian ethics, that word is *love*. We have encountered it several times already. We met it first in the context of a warning (in chap. 4): Be careful for motifs, and don't make love the be-all and end-all of ethics, losing sight of the other commandments that God has given. God not only gave the love commandment, but also told us what love should intend. The subject of love arose in chapter 5, when we were dealing with the unity of the commandments. This unity lies in the love required. No commandment can really be fulfilled if love is lacking. Therefore, it is obvious why we need to discuss this theme.

Scripture calls love *the great commandment* (Matt. 22:38). We must love God and our neighbor as ourselves. No greater commandment exists than this (Mark 12:31). Jesus proclaims the love command as *a new commandment* (John 13:34). Elsewhere love is called *the fulfilling of the law,* as we have seen. Why is it called that? Because love does no evil to one's neighbor (Rom. 13:8, 10).

Are not such formulations strong enough to allow us to conclude that our moral travel can be guided merely by the compass of love? Can we not say with Augustine: Love, and do what you please? (Augustine, *Ep. Joan.* VII:5, quoted by Fletcher 1966, 79; Fletcher points out that Augustine's Latin original does not say, as is often suggested, *ama et fac quod vis* [Love with desire and do what you please], but *dilige et quod vis, fac* [Love with care and then what you will, do]; Fletcher adds, "It was not antinomianism"). In a moment, I will return to the question of love as motif, but for now let's look at love as the *only* motif driving us toward proper decisions.

Especially in the Christianized form of *situation ethics*, we encounter love as the only necessary norm. By situation ethics, we understand that system of ethics which wishes to specify our moral conduct entirely on the basis of the situation. Universal commandments do not enter the discussion. Every time anew the person must make a free decision on the basis of the specific situation.

Situation ethics received a powerful stimulus from existentialist philosophy, which views man not as bound, but as free, always free to choose and thus to realize himself.

For Joseph Fletcher, whose book *Situation Ethics* aims to present a Christian form of situation ethics, there is but one intrinsic value. An intrinsic value is one that inherently possesses the quality of being "good" in an absolute sense, independent of every circumstance. For Fletcher, that intrinsic value is love. He acknowledges that love itself cannot be deduced by reason from the situation. But he claims that that is true also when we ascribe to something else the status of highest good, such as pleasure, which serves as the highest good in hedonism. Fletcher openly acknowledges that every moral judgment or value judgment constitutes an axiom or a presupposition. You don't simply come up with a premise to be proved, but with a decision already made. He echoes Bernard of Clairvaux, "I love because I love" (*amo quia amo*). The norm of love provides all that Fletcher needs. He wants nothing of rules or laws that people feel obligated to obtain from nature or from Scripture. Beyond love, everything is *extrinsically* determined, which means that nothing other than love is inherently good or evil. Beyond love, according to Fletcher, nothing *is* good or evil, but something can *become* good or evil, depending on the situation.

Fletcher himself provides a clear example to illustrate the notions of "intrinsic" and "extrinsic" value. He tells of a German woman held prisoner by the Soviets in Ukraine. Her husband had returned from the battlefront to Berlin, and after weeks of searching had found their children. In their pitiful situation of hunger, chaos, and fear, they desperately needed their mother. But this woman could be released from the prison camp only if she were pregnant. In that condition, she would be sent back to Germany, because she would have become too much trouble for the Soviets. The woman chose that route, with the help of a camp guard, out of love for her husband and children. A clear example! For Fletcher, adultery is not sin, as long as it is motivated by love (Fletcher 1966, 57–68, 164–65). Therefore, adultery is not inherently or intrinsically evil. It can become evil, depending on the circumstances. But the woman's adultery, in Fletcher's example, is not to be evaluated as evil, but as good. Anything motivated by love, in any situation, is intrinsically good.

We might think also of Sonia, the character in Dostoevsky's novel *Crime and Punishment*. Motivated by love for her family, Sonia became a prostitute. She rendered this sacrifice in order to keep her family alive. The German theologian Helmut Thielicke keeps open the possibility of approving her conduct. According to him, the New Testament teaches us that prostitution constitutes an impediment to the Holy Spirit's working in us (1 Cor. 6:9–20). This was as much an impediment as eating at the table of demons, spoken of in 1 Corinthians 10:21. But Thielicke is still unwilling to condemn Sonia's conduct. She may well have broken the letter of the law, but such conduct is forbidden only when a person permits himself or herself to be enslaved by such prostitution. "All things are lawful for me, but I will not be brought under the power of any" (1 Cor. 6:12). Thielicke claims that because she was driven by love, Sonia did not put herself under the dominion of idols, but remained free (Thielicke 1979a, 88–89).

We could imagine other situations where a wife deceives her husband and thereby causes only misery. Those instances of adultery would not be characterized as loving. In such cases, Fletcher would call adultery an evil and not a good.

YEAST AND DOUGH

Is love really sufficient as the only norm for our conduct? To show how impossible that is, permit me to mention a couple of objections.

The simple fact that human society is very complex renders it impossible to maintain love as the only norm. Someone has rightly observed that even if all people were good and their conduct were motivated only by love, we would still need traffic regulations and rules of commerce (jurist Peter Noll, via Hendrik van Oyen, in Veenhof 1978, 71).

In the second place, it is not true that each new situation is exceptional and requires brand-new analysis of a brand-new action. And fortunately so! For who of us would not become exhausted if with every action we had to wonder again what was right? Many moral actions proceed automatically, because many situations are virtually identical. Even the exceptional situations that Fletcher provides as illustrations occur repeatedly and can thus be generalized. Amid all the differences in situations, there is so much similarity that we can construct universal rules for our conduct. So commands and laws are not foreign at all, but inescapable. Moreover, if you take situation ethics to its logical conclusion, then there would be no courts, for how could a court function without laws? And how could there be laws without somewhat similar situations within which such laws could be applied?

In the third place, even though it is true that love is the great commandment, and that without love we are nothing (1 Cor. 13:1–13), neither of these truths means that we can envision love *apart from* the commandments. Love itself is a commandment (Matt. 22:37–40; John 13:34), and occasionally love is listed alongside other commands (or virtues), as in 1 Timothy 4:12 ("Let no one despise your youth, but be an example to the believers in word, in conduct, in love, in spirit, in faith, in purity") and in 1 Timothy 6:11 ("But you, O man of God, flee these things and pursue righteousness, godliness, faith, love, patience, gentleness"). Love nowhere stands in opposition to the commandment. In fact, Jesus says, "If you keep My commandments, you will abide in My love, just as I have kept My Father's commandments and abide in His love" (John 15:10). Whoever keeps God's commandments or keeps His Word (which means the same thing), God's love is perfected in him (1 John 2:3–5). On one occasion, Paul can write that faith works through love (Gal. 5:6), and on another that love comes down to keeping God's commandments (1 Cor. 7:19). Loving God consists in keeping His commands (1 John 5:3), or walking according to His commands (2 John 6). We may summarize it concisely this way: love is indeed the *realization* of the law, but not the *replacement* of the law (Schrage 1961, 255–56).

But now let's turn the matter around. If love is not the only command, and if love cannot function well, apart from the other commands, then neither can those other commands function well, apart from love. Love surpasses all those other commands. How can we describe the exceptional character of love? Love is the fulfillment of the law (Rom. 13:10). This must surely mean that without love, there can be no genuine, full obedience. Anyone who supposes that he can satisfy any of God's commandments without love falls into legalism, nomianism, or formalism. Whoever loves, writes Paul, does his neighbor no harm (Rom. 13:9–10), which seems to indicate that we do injure our neighbor whenever we try to obey the commandment of God without love. For our geographical orientation, we need a map and a compass. If we liken the commandments to a map, then love is the compass. Or to use another figure, love and law are related like yeast and dough. The first must permeate the second if you want good bread.

Jesus called love the great commandment, as well as a new commandment (John 13:34). That does not mean that love replaces the commandments. The command to love was "new" in a particular sense. It could also have been called an old commandment. For when Jesus formulated the dual commandment to love God and to love our neighbor (Matt. 22:37–40), He was echoing what could be found in the Old Testament already. Leviticus 19:18 says to "love your neighbor as yourself," and Deuteronomy 6:5 says to "love the LORD your God with all your heart, and with all your soul, and with all your might." But the *newness* of love lies in Jesus Himself: "A new commandment I give to you, that you love one another; *as I have loved you, that you also love one another*"—this is the precise wording of John 13:34.

We learn to know the special quality of love in Christ, as we take into account how He loved us. The mutual love among the disciples must correspond to Christ's own love, which surpasses all other love. He surrendered Himself to death for them and for us. The command to love owes its peculiar glow to Christ. Through His own life and death, love has obtained an invincible power. Only the sacrifice of Christ makes genuine love possible. The command to love is very old, but its power has reached an insurmountable height in the love of Jesus Christ. That is what is new about the old. We have already seen that we cannot speak about the commands of God apart from Christ. The very same thing applies to love. To see a picture of genuine love, look to Christ.

Can we call love the highest norm? Dutch ethicist W. H. Velema would rather not. For then we introduce a hierarchy into the commandments. Then we get commandments that must occasionally yield to the highest norm of love. Velema believes that the commandment easily becomes devalued for the sake of love. This is why he writes that love does not swallow up justice. What he means is that the commandment is obeyed out of love, and through love justice comes fully into its own (Velema 1979, 117).

I agree with him in large part, because we must not play love against the (other) commandments, as I have already explained. Nevertheless, I have no objection to calling love the highest norm. For Scripture calls love the great commandment, and no other commandment is described as being the fulfillment of the law, that is, the fulfillment of all the other commandments. Occasionally loving God and our neighbor can require us to disobey others, or tell lies, as we shall see in chapter 10.

Moreover, love often leads us to soften our judgment about others who have transgressed God's commandment. We tend to judge the German woman prisoner in the concentration camp (Fletcher's example) and Sonia (Dostoevsky) less harshly than other women who deceive their husbands or become prostitutes. Thereby we do not yet approve the behavior of the German woman or of Sonia, but we do sense what Paul is saying about love: love takes no account of evil (1 Cor. 13:5 ASV). Evil remains evil, but the command to love can do what no other commandment can do: cover evil and not assign blame.

WHAT YOU WISH OTHERS TO DO TO YOU . . .

What is said about love we read also concerning what we call the Golden Rule, found in Matthew 7:12: "Therefore, whatever you want men to do to you, do also to them, for this is the Law and the Prophets." Incidentally, the Golden Rule was known, apart from its connection with "the Law and the Prophets," in ancient India, China, and Greece. Nevertheless, just like love, the Golden Rule is called in Scripture the fulfillment of the Law and the Prophets. Surely this means that the Golden Rule and love have something to do with one another. And that is what we shall see.

But first we should say that, like love, the Golden Rule cannot function well, apart from the other commandments. Taken by itself, the Golden Rule could be interpreted in various mistaken ways. We could interpret it *egoistically*. Proceeding from our own feelings about what is acceptable or unacceptable, we could imagine what we would want another person to do. Suppose that someone refuses to show another any benevolence because he himself does not want the other to show him benevolence! For Immanuel Kant, that was reason enough to scrap the Golden Rule. With an eye to the Golden Rule, a criminal could say to the judge, "Would you want me to condemn you, if you were standing in my place? Well then, you shouldn't condemn me!" A man who isn't too scrupulous about marital fidelity could justify his wicked ways by declaring permission for his wife to hang around with other men. If we put the Golden Rule into a straitjacket, then we can reach the strange conclusions I have mentioned. But most people will realize that it was never intended for such an egoistic interpretation.

You could also interpret the Rule in a *utilitarian* way, in the sense of doing to others what you wish them to do to you, *so that* they will do what you wish! This would be a kind of "I give to you so that you give to me" (in Latin, *do ut des*). I'll scratch your back, so you'll scratch mine. In this case, we are not focusing exclusively on our own self-interest, since we are considering the other person too, but then simply to advance our own position. It seems that the Rule can be used in quite different ways, but clearly Jesus did not intend us to go in this direction.

You could also maintain the Rule in a more friendly way by interpreting it *axiologically*. Here we might evaluate our neighbor's conduct neither by starting with ourselves (egoism) nor by ending with ourselves (utilitarianism), but far more objectively, on the basis of values that rank very high in our society. We would then tend to identify evil more clearly and prominently in terms of others who mistreat us than in terms of our mistreatment of them. The sliver in another's eye is more quickly identified than the beam in our own eye (Matt. 7:3–5). For that reason, it is good to use the measure applied to others for testing our own conduct.

With that last interpretation of the Rule, we are not far from the truth. For this use of the Golden Rule does point us to a norm that is not identical to the Rule itself, one that comes to us from a slightly different source. When we take Matthew 7:12 seriously, that source is easily identified. The norm is indicated in the Rule itself: the Law and the Prophets. Just like love, the Golden Rule can include commandments, but it does not produce those commandments.

We have already seen that the Golden Rule and love must somehow be related, because the same thing is said about both. The content of the Law and the Prophets can be comprehended both in the command to love and in the Golden Rule. Why? Note the words "whatever you want men to do to you." Although we are often strict toward others, we prefer that they be lenient toward us. We prefer that people treat us with sympathy and compassion. Said another way, although we often treat others without love, we expect love from them toward us. For that reason we can quite accurately restate the Golden Rule this way: Show toward your neighbors the love you expect from them! Our feelings regarding what we would like from others are very well developed. If the reverse is also true, we will then demonstrate love in its full capacity.

SELF-LOVE

The great commandment says that we must love God with all our heart, soul, and mind. The second, like the first, says, "You shall love your neighbor as yourself" (Matt. 22:37–40). Do the words "as yourself" imply that God commands us to love ourselves? That conclusion is not obvious, for Matthew 22:37–40 is talking not about three, but about two commands. It says, "You shall love your neighbor *as* yourself," not "*and* yourself"! The words "as yourself" do not contain a duty of self-love, but rather rest on observable fact. We do in fact love ourselves, and the intensity of that self-love can serve as a measurement for our love toward our neighbor. The intensity of a person's love of himself should be the intensity of his love for his neighbor.

Nowhere does Scripture present a command to love oneself; rather, it points us to self-denial. Whoever loves his life will lose it (John 12:25). Love does not seek itself (1 Cor. 13:5). Loving oneself is presented in Scripture as something negative, as we note from Paul's warning that in the last days people will be "lovers of themselves" (*philautoi*, 2 Tim. 3:2).

Loving our neighbors as ourselves is embodied also in the Golden Rule, which we have just considered. That Rule also involves the command to love your neighbor, but not to love yourself. The point is simply that what we ourselves would like to receive provides a clear indication of what we should grant others. Once more, we are usually very sensitive about what we have coming to us and where we have been short-changed. Take that, then, as the standard for knowing how to love the other person well. In a concrete instance, Paul uses similar reasoning: "He who loves his wife loves himself. For no one ever hated his own flesh, but nourishes and cherishes it" (Eph. 5:28–29). Those words give us an excellent picture of our self-love—not as a command, but as a fact. The command might even require us to hate our life in this world in order to preserve it for eternity (John 12:25)!

Augustine, Bernard of Clairvaux, Thomas Aquinas, and others did indeed speak of a command to love ourselves. In order to deal fairly with their viewpoint, we should not think that they were defending an egoistic self-love. Bernard of Clairvaux, for example, spoke of a ladder of self-love with the following rungs:

(1) love for its own sake, pure self-love;
(2) love toward God for its own sake, again, a form of self-love, because man needs God in order to become better;
(3) love toward God for God's sake, something that is no longer self-love; and
(4) love toward oneself for God's sake, something that is indeed self-love, but then a form that in this life is only partially attainable. This requires our complete absorption into God. (Bernard, *De diligendo Deo* 987–88)

The last or fourth stage has nothing to do with naked egoism. But the question is whether it precludes a refined egoism. This kind of love is inconceivable apart from the mysticism in which the person is taken up entirely into God. Loving oneself and loving God are in fact the same. In a harmonious, sinless world it may be possible to imagine love toward God completely corresponding with love toward oneself, although even then the boundary between God and man would remain intact. But in the world we live in today, such is not possible. Moreover, in the dual command Christ gave us, self-love is not directly tied to love toward God, but to love toward our neighbor. Would we be able to say that loving oneself and loving our neighbor must ideally be entirely identical? Should you love yourself for your neighbor's sake? Whatever our answer, this view is not in Matthew 22, where we read simply, "Love your neighbor *as* yourself."

Self-love is not commanded in Scripture, but neither is it forbidden. Paul says that nobody hates his own flesh, but nourishes and cherishes it. He does not say this with a dismissive tone. Nor should we read such a tone into Jesus' words. *If* we must love others because they are creatures of God, the same goes for loving ourselves. Nourishing and cherishing our flesh is the opposite of hating ourselves. Self-respect and self-love are natural and proper. Jesus' summons to deny ourselves comes always in terms of our relationships to God and our neighbor. If we should face the choice between pleasing ourselves and pleasing God, then we must choose the path of self-denial. Or if we should face the choice between pleasing ourselves and offering help to our neighbor, then again we must choose the path of self-denial. The impropriety is not that we love ourselves, but that in our self-love we go too far and love ourselves more than we love God and our neighbor.

So we need not reject self-respect and self-love. Even as we are related to God and our neighbor, so we are related to ourselves. We will develop this further in chapter 8, when we take up the matter of conscience. The notion of conscience makes it clear that a person exists in relation to himself or herself. But that relation does not yield a third command to love. A person may properly love himself, something he does without needing a command to do it. Our self-love can even serve to indicate the intensity with which we must love our neighbor. Self-love contains much that is good because it contains much that is natural. We observe this when people become psychologically ill and consider their own lives worthless or even hate living at all. At that point, it is not fitting to summon them to self-denial; rather, a way must be found for them to recover their self-love. But the healthy person, who can be appealed to ethically, knows that he usually loves himself instead of God and his neighbor. As long as that is the case, two, not three, commandments apply: Love God and love your neighbor as yourself, with self-denial.

We could state it somewhat paradoxically: where the dual love for God and for our neighbor is found in our lives, there self-love develops fully. This is the same paradox contained in Jesus' words, "Whoever loses his life for My sake will find it" (Matt. 16:25). This double vision does not alienate a person from himself, but is precisely what allows him to attain his created purpose.

THREE FORMS OF LOVE

Healthy love colors all our conduct. Love can be expressed in various ways, but it is universally indispensable. Here we can employ the three forms of love that H. van Oyen distinguishes. He does so with the help of three Greek words: *agapē*, *philia*, and *eros* (Van Oyen 1952, 115–215).

Agapē is the love of surrender, love that takes seriously the demand of self-denial that belongs to the imitation of Christ. It always embodies a choice. I refer here to Mark 12:28–34, where a scribe asks Jesus which is the first of all the commandments. Jesus answers, "The first of all the commandments is: 'Hear, O Israel, the LORD our God, the LORD is one. And you shall love the LORD your God with all your heart, with all your soul, with all your mind, and with all your strength.' This is the first commandment. And the second, like it, is this: 'You shall love your neighbor as yourself.' There is no other commandment greater than these" (Mark 12:29–31). The two parts of the quotation from Deuteronomy 6, about the one Lord and the command to love Him, belong together. Love is choosing for the one God, the one Lord Jesus, that one name above all names.

Choosing for God and for the neighbor He places in our path means that we do *not* choose for the desire of the flesh, the desire of the eyes, and the pride of life. For in that case we are choosing for the world. But if we love the world, the love of the Father is not in us (1 John 2:15–16). Our love for our Father is not something automatic, for often it goes against our own desires and preferences. Recall the command to love our enemies and to pray for those who persecute us (Matt. 5:44).

The second form of love Van Oyen explains with another Greek word for love: *philia*. That word describes love for the ordering of life. It holds ordinary life together: kinship, friendship, a society characterized by fairness.

What Van Oyen means by this form of love we find already with Augustine. Love aims at peace among men, at an ordered unity where we intend no injury and where we benefit our neighbor wherever possible (Augustine, *De civitate Dei*

19.14). In society, love and justice must be united. This is what we see when governments defend the needy, the oppressed, and the persecuted (Jer. 22:3, 15–17; Ps. 72).

Thus, Van Oyen does not separate love from public life. Love involves not only intimate relationships (I-Thou), but also respect for order and justice in society, where we deal with government and other public institutions. Love must regulate all of life. In the house of life, love does not occupy its own little room, nor does it wish to be treated as a guest; rather, it desires to furnish the whole house with its presence (Ridderbos 1975, 111). Put crassly, the sword of the state, including its waging of a just war, can be seen as an instrument of love. Luther made such a claim when he considered the struggle that people of his day waged against the revolutionary Turks (see Thielicke 1979b, 462). Protecting our own borders is an act of love that the government ought to perform on behalf of its own citizens. This conviction prevents us from construing love only in terms of the Sermon on the Mount and not in terms of the discussion of the sword of government in Romans 13. There we read that government exists in service to God, *for our good* (Rom. 13:4). There is no reason for denying that the good conduct of government is a form of love, even though it is far less personal than the more direct relationships among people.

The third form of love that Van Oyen distinguishes is *eros*, another Greek word for love. This love is experienced in sensual attraction and procreating new life. This love has everything to do with desire and affection. In fact, Van Oyen expands this form to include the nonsexual arena of life expressed in bringing forth culture and technology.

Perhaps there are other and better distinctions than the

ones Van Oyen offers. But any distinctions we employ must show that love covers the entire domain of human living.

Literature

Fletcher, Joseph. 1966. *Situation ethics: The new morality*. Philadelphia: Westminster Press.

Ridderbos, S. J. 1975. *Ethiek van het liefdegebod.* Kampen: Kok.

Schrage, W. 1961. *Die konkreten Einzelgebote in der paulinischen Paränese.* Gütersloh: Mohn.

Thielicke, Helmut. 1979a. *Theological ethics.* Vol. 1, *Foundations.* Edited by William H. Lazareth. Philadelphia: Fortress.

Thielicke, Helmut. 1979b. *Theological ethics.* Vol. 2, *Politics.* Edited by William H. Lazareth. Philadelphia: Fortress.

Van Oyen, H. 1952. *Evangelische Ethik: Grundlagen.* Basel: Reinhardt.

Veenhof, Jan. 1978. *Geist und Liebe: Die systematischen Voraussetzungen der Ethik Hendrik van Oyens.* Amsterdam: Rodopi.

Velema, W. H. 1979. De liefde is de vervulling van de wet. In *Uw knecht hoort. Theologische opstellen aangeboden aan W. Kremer, J. Van Genderen, en B. J. Oosterhoff.* Amsterdam: Bolland.

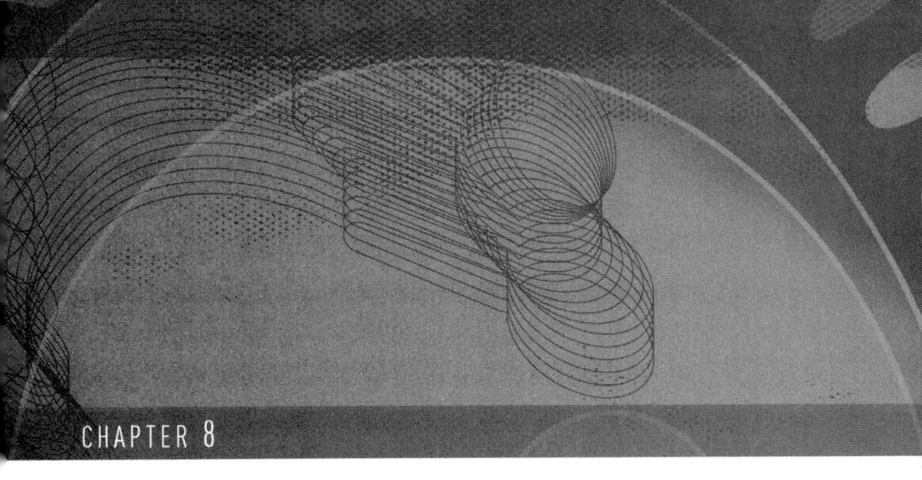

CHAPTER 8

Conscience

AN ANCIENT DISTINCTION

We have seen that love, all by itself, cannot provide sufficient guidance for our moral conduct. We need something else. As we have seen, love fulfills the law, but does not replace God's commandments. Something else is also often nominated to be a moral guide: the *conscience*. An enormous amount has been written, especially in earlier times, about the function of the conscience. And even today we occasionally ask ourselves the important question whether our conscience permits us to do what we want to do. But what exactly do we mean by our "conscience"?

In the Middle Ages, a distinction was drawn between the synteresis and the conscience. The term *synteresis* has a peculiar origin. In his commentary on Ezekiel, the church father Jerome (*ca.* 347–419) wrote about the four living creatures that appear in chapter 1: a man, a lion, an ox, and an eagle. Jerome used the imagery of these four creatures to construct his anthropology or view of human personality. The man, the lion, and the ox referred, in turn, to human understanding, will, and desire, whereas the eagle hovering above them all was the conscience enlightened by God to correct the understanding, the will, and the desire. The word *synteresis* is related to the Greek word *syntērein*, which means "to preserve." Thus, the synteresis can be seen as the preserver and protector of the divine commandments in human life.

The word *synteresis* lay dormant a long time, until it acquired a very significant function during the Middle Ages. In that era, it came to refer to the light of nature that inclined man toward the good and restrained him from the evil. The synteresis was even portrayed as the human capacity for knowing in an infallible way the fundamental principles of conduct.

But if man was equipped with such a noble capacity, how could he still err? The fault lay, according to theologians, not with the synteresis, which after all was infallible, but with the application of the synteresis to everyday matters. That application was a function of the conscience (in Latin, *conscientia*). In his conscience, man could err.

What was absent from Jerome's thinking we find later in the thinking of Alexander Halesius, Thomas Aquinas, and others, namely, that the conscience embodies two elements, an infallible core known as the synteresis, and a fallible application known as the conscience. This application, in the opinion of theologians, proceeded along the route of the practical syllogism. A syllogism contains two judgments, the more comprehensive one being contained in the major premise and the less comprehensive one in the minor premise, followed by a conclusion. We can illustrate this with some examples.

MAJOR PREMISE: All sinners must die. (Each person knows this; the sentence of death on the basis of sin is apprehended by the synteresis.)

MINOR PREMISE: I am a sinner.

CONCLUSION: I must die. (This conclusion applies to me what the synteresis knows as a generalization, and belongs to the function of the conscience.)

Here is one more illustration:

MAJOR PREMISE: "As the LORD lives, the man who has done this shall surely die!" (David said this to Nathan [2 Sam. 12:5]. The synteresis indicated it to him.)

MINOR PREMISE: "You are the man!" (Nathan said this to David [2 Sam. 12:7].)

CONCLUSION: "I have sinned against the LORD," and I am thus a child of death. (This was the verdict of David's conscience [2 Sam. 12:13].)

The synteresis cannot err, people argued throughout the Middle Ages, but the conscience can err, since a person often mistakenly applies the universal principle to the particular case. Here, however, the church stepped in to offer help. In the confessional, clergymen could speak the decisive word in all cases of conscience, in the so-called *casus conscientiae*.

Here we have one of the sources of casuistry. A person can err, but fortunately there are ecclesiastical specialists who can show us the way out of our moral dilemmas with the help of their manuals of casuistry!

Not only during the Middle Ages, but long thereafter people continued to speak of the human synteresis as an infallible core. Protestant scholastics borrowed the distinction between synteresis and conscience, a distinction that has functioned until very recently. (In fact, as recently as 1937 a theological dissertation, presented at the Free University of Amsterdam, argued that conscience consisted of a core or a root that is not part of the creation [Prins 1937, 508].)

WHAT IS THE CONSCIENCE?

By "conscience" I refer to *that authority within a person which places him before his own future or past decisions and which renders a verdict, whether of approval or disapproval, upon those decisions.* This definition says nothing yet about the content of conscience. For that content can be quite diverse. Here we are saying simply that a person is a self-conscious being, and that he renders a verdict about his own conduct, either beforehand or afterward. These two moments (before and after) are indicated by the classical phrases *conscientia antecedens* (evaluating future decisions) and *conscientia consequens* (evaluating past decisions).

We do not meet the term *conscience* in the Old Testament. Naturally, the capacity itself is present there. What we refer to as "conscience" the Old Testament refers to as "the heart." When God threatens to punish His people by sending them into captivity, He warns those who are left that He "will send faintness *into their hearts* in the lands of their enemies; the sound of a shaken leaf shall cause them to flee" (Lev. 26:36). During their captivity, He would give them "a trembling heart" (Deut. 28:65).

Already in the Old Testament, it is evident that conscience and context, time and development, are closely intertwined. When Abimelech of Gerar was warned in a dream to keep away from Sarah, Abraham's wife, he answered that he had acted "in the integrity of my heart" (Gen. 20:5). We would say "with a clear conscience." Notice that Abimelech's conscience was not activated by the fact that he was going to take another wife. He could still do such a thing with a clear conscience, even as Abraham similarly was a polygamist (Gen. 25:1–6). Today our consciences would burn if we acted that way! Our consciences revolt against polygamy. Here already we see that conscience does not have an unalterable content.

In the New Testament, where we do encounter a word for "conscience" (*syneidēsis*), it is even more evident that the conscience is not a constant entity, but can function quite diversely, either well or partially or mistakenly. Paul can say, "For I know nothing against myself"—that is, "my conscience is clear"—to which he immediately adds, "yet I am not justified by this; but He who judges me is the Lord" (1 Cor. 4:4). In my conscience, I may well be unaware of any wrongdoing, but that does not yet justify me before God. Conscience is a relative thing, something that always remains subordinated to God's evaluation.

In addition, what the New Testament says about the *weak* conscience confirms that the human conscience is both variable and fallible. There are people, Paul says, who are not yet free from idols. For that reason, they do not dare eat food that is sold in the markets of Corinth, meat that has first been sacrificed in pagan temples. Were they to eat this food, their consciences, weak as they are, would be defiled (1 Cor. 8:7, 10, 12). One person's conscience could handle it, but another's could not (1 Cor. 10:28–29; for a broader discussion of this question, see Kloosterman 1991).

Paul tells Timothy that the consciences of apostate believers have been seared with a hot iron (1 Tim. 4:2). They have a *bad* conscience and act contrary to everything they had once learned. Both one's mind and one's conscience can be defiled (Titus 1:15). From this fact, we see that one's conscience will not remain untouched if one's mind is corrupted.

So human conscience has many facets. Surely we should not view conscience as a sacred—let alone infallible—capacity. The conscience is not a temple where God and man meet. For that reason, it is less useful to render the literal meaning of the words *syneidēsis* and *conscientia* as "knowing with God." Such a rendering is often proposed, even by John Calvin, who calls conscience "a certain means" between God and man (*Institutes* 3.19.15). The little word "with" can just as well pertain to the person, as in "knowing with oneself," that is, being conscious of one's own deliberations and actions.

A GOOD CONSCIENCE

Especially in the nineteenth and early twentieth centuries, conscience was toppled from the elevated throne it had occupied for centuries. Two great scholars contributed significantly to that toppling: Friedrich Nietzsche (1844–1900) and Sigmund Freud (1856–1939).

In his book *On the Genealogy of Morals* (German original, 1887), Nietzsche describes the conscience as a symptom of the illness that society inflicts on man by domesticating him and suppressing his primitive vital instincts. Freud portrays the essence of man as something impersonal, as the "it" or "id." The id consists of a person's innate drives or biological instincts, all arising from the sexual urge. Within the id, the impulse of lust dominates without restraint. But the "I" or "ego" must adapt to its environment. Human drives cannot be lived out; they need to be censored. The outward expression of "libido" (those impulses aroused by the id) is hindered by commandments and prohibitions, especially those of parents. An identification develops between the ego and external authorities, especially external authority embodied in one's father. Thus, there arises within the ego itself a governing authority, called the "super ego," which evaluates critically all the actions of an individual, rewarding with a clear conscience or punishing with a guilty conscience. The super ego is the incarnation of morality. The impulse of lust is engaged in an eternal struggle against the inescapable claims of reality. The ego is endangered from two sides with the threat of disintegration: on the one hand, by the impulses of the id, which strive for supremacy, and on the other hand by the restraint of the super ego, which denies the id its wishes. Freud views the conscience as the guilt feeling produced by the ego living amid the tension between the id and the super ego.

Fundamental to this perspective is an anthropology that a Christian cannot accept. If we did accept it, we would in turn have to believe that the beginning of all things is a chaos of human urges. Freud's morality has no room for a person being created in God's image and less room for man's fall into sin as the fountain of all misery, including psychological misery.

However, what Nietzsche and Freud have taught us clearly is that the content of human consciences differs widely. We cannot really speak of *the* conscience, for that doesn't exist. Something that one person cannot find in his heart to do, another person does with a quiet conscience. Our upbringing and society's influence are very influential in forming our consciences. We can see that in the altered moral climate since about 1960. Actions that were disapproved before that, like abortion and homosexual behavior, are nowadays simply accepted by many people.

Can we, then, even speak of a clear conscience or a guilty conscience? Yes, of course, but then we must bind human conscience closely to the content of Scripture. A clear conscience is a clear conscience before God. This is why Paul could say that before God he has a completely clear conscience about his public conduct (Acts 23:1). He made a practice of having a pure conscience before God and others (Acts 24:16). For him, a good conscience goes along with an unfeigned faith (1 Tim. 1:5; cf. also 1:19 and 3:9). You can count on having a clear conscience if you desire to live right (Heb. 13:18). We must obey the civil government not only "because of wrath but also for conscience' sake" (Rom. 13:5). This means that we must be subject, not only in order to escape the government's exercise of punishment, but also because God asks this of us. A clear conscience is always coupled with obedience to God's commandments.

I have already indicated that a clear conscience does not yet justify us before God. But in spite of that, we can still continue speaking of a clear conscience. For Scripture itself does so. With regard to a multitude of matters, we may be so bold as to declare that we have done them with a clear conscience. In so doing, we are declaring that we are prepared to give an account of our behavior before God and man. But a clear conscience cannot live without grace. A clear conscience does not "justify" us before God (1 Cor. 4:4). Even a Christian conscience is not constant, but shifting. Recall the "weak" conscience of people who are upright Christians, but who can still possess a narrow vision. Such Christians in Corinth definitely ate no sacrificial food, and nowadays we have Christians who definitively reject a new hymnal or permit no television in the house. At the same time, other Christians are so free that they attribute these and similar convictions to a weak conscience.

On the basis of all of this, we may conclude that an appeal to conscience is never the final word. Conscience, too, is subject to the Word of God and needs to be cleansed by the blood of Christ.

DEALING WITH APPEALS TO CONSCIENCE

Our consciences are not infallible. Therefore, we cannot rely upon our consciences as if we needed no other guide to locate the proper course of conduct. This is not to relegate conscience to an insignificant role. God lays claim to conscience, not only for Christians, but for non-Christians as well. Again we recall Romans 2:15, where we read about the work of the law written in the hearts of pagans, "their conscience also bearing witness, and between themselves their thoughts accusing or else excusing them" on the Day of Judgment. God's law makes such a deep impression that, willingly or unwillingly, it keeps on affecting the non-Christian. Many people simply cannot eradicate it from their conscience. And that fact will appear on the Day of Judgment, when human consciences begin to speak. Certainly a person can so oppose God's revelation that his conscience no longer functions. It can be deadened, even to the point of denying God's existence. However, these distortions of conscience should not lead us to dismiss the voice of conscience as unimportant. To appeal to conscience is to appeal to one's deepest convictions. Even if we do not agree with such convictions, we may not disregard them. Recall that the apostle Paul, although agreeing with the view of the strong believers that permitted eating food sacrificed in a pagan temple, nevertheless dealt respectfully with the consciences of Christians whose convictions differed from his own.

Occasionally, significant consequences result from appealing to conscience. Consider the objections to military service when the government conscripts people for such duty. There have always been Christians who were convinced in their conscience that they could never serve in an army. The commandment "Thou shalt not kill" prevented them from entering the military, because they refused to take up arms against another human being. This conviction is not shared by all Christians, including myself. But that does not mean that this conviction was not and is not held seriously. We know of testimonies of Christians from the first centuries who refused to enter military service and had to surrender their very lives for their conviction. (For a more extensive discussion of the various motives that led Christians to refuse to serve in the Roman military, see Douma 1988, 48–78.) These testimonies are so moving that we have no difficulty believing in the genuineness of their conscientious objections. It was not too long ago that we heard the conscientious objections of young people who objected not to any and every war, but to nuclear war. But this is a case where it remains difficult to find such conscientious objections convincing. Why would a person oppose one kind of war and not another? Still more unclear is the position of someone who opposes any form of military service, but has no problem with participating in a forceful overthrow of a regime that is oppressing its own citizens. We may rightly expect conscientious objections to be consistent. You cannot be willing to permit tomorrow what you reject today. For in that case, something Godfried Bomans once observed becomes relevant: many owe their clear consciences to their faulty memories!

Literature

Douma, J. 1988. *Gewapende vrede*. 4th ed. Kampen: Van den Berg.

Kloosterman, Nelson D. 1991. *Scandalum infirmorum: Christian liberty and neighbor love in the church*. Neerlandia, Alberta: Inheritance Publications.

Prins, P. 1937. *Het geweten*. Delft: Meinema.

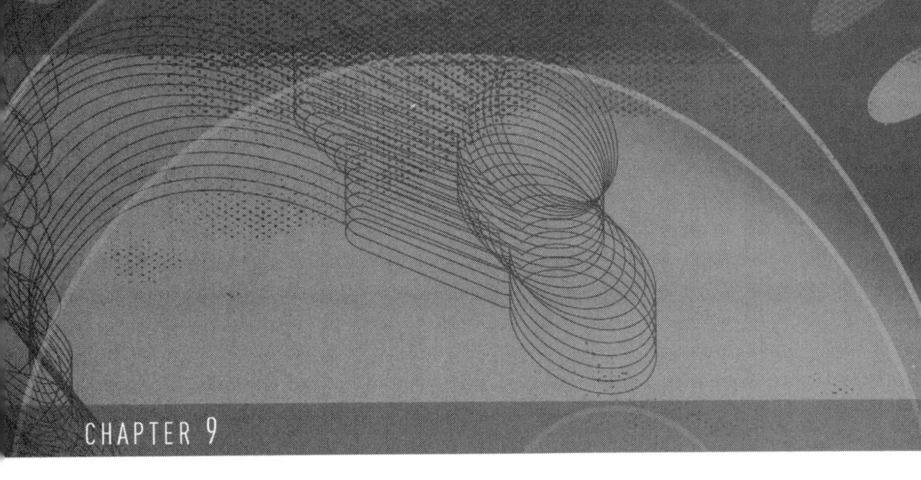

Are There Adiaphora?

THE ISSUE

We observed already in chapter 4 that Scripture has no precept or prohibition for many actions that we either commit or omit. It became clear that in maturity we may discern what really matters (Phil. 1:9–10). Bound to Scripture and led by the Spirit, we decide in freedom, because we are not slaves, but children in God's house.

In this chapter, I want to provide more content to the notion of *freedom*. I do so in terms of an old ethical issue known by the term *adiaphora*. (For a more extensive discussion of this subject and for a bibliography, see Douma 1974.)

What is meant by this term? By "adiaphora" we understand *those things and actions that people call neither good nor evil*. You can either accept or reject such things; you can either do or not do such actions; but they are not subject to a judgment of being good or evil. The Greek word *adiaphora* means "indifferent things," which are therefore characterized as neither good nor evil. The term *adiaphora* is also rendered by the descriptive phrase "morally neutral." These things fall between good and evil, between what is absolutely commanded and what is absolutely forbidden. They occupy a domain where "Thou shalt" or "Thou shalt not" do not apply, but where one may freely act in commission or omission.

Are there adiaphora? That is the question of this chapter. Christians disagree on this matter. Let's first investigate why people affirm or deny the existence of adiaphora.

First, the affirmative. There are adiaphora. Don't all Christians persistently do things that—and this they assume to be self-evident—have nothing to do with our relationship with God? For example, would it not be morbid to seek the will of God, as we are taking a stroll, in order to determine whether we should turn left or right? Would not living become unbearable if at every point we needed to ask whether we were living scrupulously before God? Suppose that in view of their extravagance, we were to condemn pastries; do we not run the risk, in our scrupulosity, that we will have to give up coffee and tea as well? Will we not also be wondering whether our daily meals could not be more plain; should we eat only what we need to stay alive? A Christian ethic must defend Christian freedom, and therefore protect various choices that a Christian may make or not, without turning them into an ethical problem. Fortunately, adiaphora do indeed exist, for otherwise life would become burdensome.

But others deny the existence of adiaphora. They argue that what some people call "nonessential" actions and choices often have far-reaching consequences. And once you accept the existence of adiaphora, you have taken your first step down the slippery slope. You will slide easily to the bottom of this slope by leaving more and more decisions to personal preference and finally exempting all of life from obedience to Christ. If, as a Christian, you are truly a slave of Christ, there is not one moment when you are your own master.

The reader will sense already that this issue of adiaphora quickly focuses on what is permissible and impermissible in the area of entertainment. May I dance, play cards, smoke, use alcohol, take an expensive vacation, and the like? Are all of these forbidden by God, or is this an arena where the Christian may decide freely, because it involves "morally neutral" matters?

A TERM FROM THE STOICS

The roots of the concept of adiaphora are located in the philosophical movement of the Stoics. The concept was forged in that school of thought. The Stoics identified a third zone between those of the good and the evil, namely, the zone of the adiaphora. Everything that yields neither gain nor loss they called adiaphora, which covered a lot of things. Life, health, pleasure, physical beauty, strength, wealth, a good reputation, and a noble ancestry belonged to this arena. But so did death, sickness, pain, physical ugliness, weakness, poverty, a bad reputation, and an inferior lineage. Why? Because each of these can lead in two directions. Wealth can be used rightly and wrongly. Poverty can induce a person to thievery, but it can also purify him morally. And something that we can use either rightly or wrongly cannot itself be called a good or a bad thing. Even life is not a good thing in itself. It may well happen that we choose suicide.

If the Stoics viewed so many things as adiaphora, what then did they actually assign to the genuinely and essentially good? For the Stoics, it came down to being free in all things. A person must accept all things—prosperity and adversity, health and sickness, even life and death—with stoical resignation. A person should be characterized by the attitude of *apatheia* (literally, "without feeling").

In fact, however, it was impossible for the Stoics to maintain the position that life and death, health and sickness, and wealth and poverty are all in the same category. It was obvious that nature induces people to strive for certain things (like life and health) and to avoid other things (like death and sickness). Even though life and health are not *essentially* good, they are nevertheless preferable to the nonpreferable things (in Greek, the *proēgmena* and the *apoproēgmena*). Guided by reason, the preferable things may be enjoyed and the nonpreferable things rejected. In addition to these, the Stoics distinguished yet a third category: the *oudetera*, literally translated as "neither of the two." These are actions that arouse neither desire nor aversion, which health and sickness, life and death, and wealth and poverty do arouse. These are absolutely neutral matters, like counting an even or odd number of hairs on someone's head, extending or retracting one's finger, or picking up or ignoring a straw.

When you reflect on these views of the Stoics, you are struck by the difference between them and the Christian faith. In the first place, you are struck by the *rationalistic* character of this ethic. Every action must be thought through, and be transparent to human reason. Each action must proceed from within and not be induced by external forces. The person who desires to be wise must display apathy and thus not express spontaneous joy or let loose with tears or become angry. Everything not directed by reason must be eradicated.

Calvin said of the Stoics that they acted foolishly because they called someone high-minded who reacted in exactly the same way in adversity and in prosperity. Scripture teaches something else. It says that those who mourn are blessed (Matt. 5:4). Jesus was troubled in spirit, even unto death (Matt. 26:38).

In the second place, notice how *individualistic* this view of adiaphora is. The human person is torn from his world, so that the world itself becomes an adiaphoron. But nothing exists by itself, no person and no world. The world that came forth from God's hand is one; all things are related to each other, and every creature has received its own form and task. The kaleidoscopic quality of God's world pales into one gray adiaphoric mass with the Stoics.

In the third place, it is not true that life and death, health and sickness, and wealth and poverty belong *inherently* to one category. We are en route to a world where there will be no room for death, sickness, and poverty. On the way there, evil things can be good for us, and good things can be bad for us. For example, recall that Scripture often points to wealth as dangerous. But the situation will change when death, sickness, and poverty will no longer appear alongside life, health, and wealth. Therefore, it is fitting that already now, during this earthly life, we not respond coldly (apathetically) to things that are good and evil. They all come from God's hand. Not one of them belongs to the adiaphora, because they are included in God's plan of mercy and love toward us.

In the fourth place, we can point to the *political barrenness* of these thoughts on adiaphora. The Stoics emphasized only the interior attitude and dismissed the thought of improving the exterior circumstances. A good illustration of this is slavery. The notion that all people are essentially alike, as the Stoics developed the idea, did not lead society straightway to dispense with slavery. After all, the living conditions of a free man or a slave are not important. What was emphasized was the person's inner attitude toward the surrounding environment. A person could fulfill his moral duty and live happily even though he was born in chains and died in them. The Christian faith, by contrast, cannot be satisfied with this dissonance between inward and outward, precisely *because* a Christian does not assign the outward to the category of adiaphora. The gospel is salt *in* the world. Christ came not only to forgive sins, but also to give sight to the blind, to feed the hungry, and to restore human lives to fruitfulness by driving out demons.

TWO DISPUTES ABOUT ADIAPHORA

It's a long road from the Stoics to the present. To relate everything said throughout the centuries on the subject of adiaphora is both impossible and unnecessary. But in order to bring out the significance of the subject a bit more clearly, I want to discuss two heated disputes about adiaphora.

The first dispute about adiaphora occurred during the time of the Reformation. The occasion was the so-called Leipzig Interim of 1548, designed to bring Roman Catholic and Lutheran theologians together. From the Lutheran side, Melanchthon, a close friend of Luther, made significant concessions to the Roman Catholics—for example, concerning confirmation, extreme unction or last rites, and many ceremonial rituals in public worship. Melanchthon believed that these were defensible concessions, since they involved adiaphora. However, the result was not unity between Lutherans and Roman Catholics, but division among Lutherans. That was to be expected. Church bells, worship candles, and clerical robes may seem to be indifferent things, but Melanchthon's opponents understood better than he did that you cannot abstract such things from their historical context. The art of abstraction, the practice of evaluating something all by itself, was driven by defenders of adiaphora to great lengths. But those matters which Melanchthon viewed as adiaphora functioned within a certain context and had a lot to do with the church's creed and with offending others, so that it was naive to identify them as adiaphora.

The second dispute about adiaphora was waged at the end of the seventeenth century, again in Lutheran circles. But now it was the Pietists who were averse to any talk about adiaphora and took up the battle against attending the opera, playing cards, dancing, and such things. They identified the wrongfulness of those activities not in the abuse, but in the very use, of them. According to these Pietists, only those actions are good that have God's honor as their goal and that are performed in faith and in the name of Christ. Actions involving humor and jest are not commanded by God, but invented by men for their own pleasure. For that reason, they are inherently sinful.

One Pietist argued that only two kinds of desire existed: desire wrought by the Holy Spirit and innate sinful desire. Another Pietist contended that a Christian can find enjoyment in a directly religious way only by contemplation, prayer, and spiritual music. Socializing must have a religious content. One should find his leisure in that kind of activity, or else only in useful activities like studying and handicrafts. What one may or may not do was stipulated precisely. Banquets were sinful, for such pleasure went beyond what was strictly necessary, and conversations at a banquet inevitably contained humor and were therefore wrong. Music, which had been given to us for holy purposes, was misused when it accompanied dancing. The stage was wrong because of its pagan origin. Even strolling was occasionally disapproved, because it could be an expression of a spirit that was not resting in God. In the orphanage of Halle, people went so far as to forbid children's games.

When we evaluate such opinions, we should not forget that the Pietists were taking a stand against the lax lifestyle of their day. That is to their credit. Nevertheless, they went too far in condemning what were sometimes very ordinary activities. For example, it is too simplistic to say that desire is either wrought by the Holy Spirit or innately sinful. This either-or analysis applies to a human life in its entirety before the judgment seat of God: Is it a life governed by the Holy Spirit, or is it a life where sin continues to exercise its dominion? But this dualism easily leads people to assign to the category of "innate sinful desire" the desires relating to the natural instincts of our senses: seeing, and finding things pretty; hearing, and enjoying music; smelling, and being attracted by the fragrance of flowers or food. A human being remains human in using the capacities of smell, taste, hearing, sight, and touch, for all of these capacities were given to us when we were created. To put it the way Calvin did, you may not rob a man of all his senses and make him a block of wood. Would the Lord have decorated flowers with such grandeur, Calvin wondered (*Institutes* 3.10.2), a splendor that catches our eyes, and not permit us to lift our eyes or use our nose to enjoy them?

We can say the same thing about entertainment and leisure. The rhythm of work and rest, of labor and leisure, remains a creational reality, even though sin can affect our manner of working and resting. To deny children in an orphanage the opportunity to play, however, is to equate the creational with the sinful.

We may not permit nature to be swallowed by sin, so that everything that involves ordinary smelling, tasting, and relaxing is considered sinful. But among the Pietists nothing was "ordinary." Everything had to have a spiritual flavor. Rather than grace healing nature, for them grace destroys nature. The Christian must be self-consciously occupied with God throughout the entire day.

But that is impossible. A farmer who wants to plow his field with straight furrows has little time for meditating about God. The same goes for someone who is busy playing a game. People stay human and do not become divine. On Sunday we must pay full attention when God speaks to us in church, but during the week we must be permitted to devote ourselves fully to the work to which this same God has called us. And what goes for work goes as well for leisure.

What is remarkable is that the Pietists, whose rejection of the concept of adiaphora was directly opposite to the view of the Stoics, came to stand right next to them when they insisted that every human action must be self-conscious and reasoned. You can find a deep rationalistic streak in the ethics of both groups, even though the outworking may have differed. The Stoics led man to turn constantly inward toward himself, while the Pietists wanted man to focus constantly upon God. Both groups, however, easily lifted man out of the relationships in which God put him in the world. The Stoics declared the world outside of man to be indifferent; the Pietists declared it to be forbidden. In both cases, the development of the human person, who with all his being is directed toward the creation, is frustrated.

NO ADIAPHORA

After this brief historical excursion, I am prepared to answer the question whether there are adiaphora. No further argument is needed to persuade us that many activities are not addressed in Scripture by way of explicit commandment. God gave man the mandate to fill and subdue the earth and rule over the animals (Gen. 1:28). But how we should be doing one thing or another is hardly treated at all. Man was prohibited from eating of the tree of the knowledge of good and evil, but he was permitted to choose in freedom from among all the other fruits (Gen. 2:16–17). In the New Testament era, the believer may marry or remain unmarried (1 Cor. 7). He may eat meat and other foods, but he may also abstain from them (Rom. 14:1; 1 Cor. 8 and 10). Special days may be observed, but one may just as permissibly ignore them (Rom. 14:5–6). Something may well be good, and the other things may be even better (1 Cor. 7:38). A word like *better* presupposes that an imposed "ought" is out of the question. Not marrying can be better than marrying, but marrying is better than burning with desire (1 Cor. 7:9). In any case, it is clear that when a person is making even very important decisions in life, he cannot appeal to a special revelation from God, but may and can discern the proper path in freedom.

To deny this in an attempt to legitimize every action with the imprimatur of "Thus saith the Lord" is to restrict Christian freedom. For the truth of the matter is that very many actions are neither commanded nor forbidden in Scripture.

But does that mean that there are adiaphora? If you understand the word literally, you will easily apply it to a *neutral zone* where man sovereignly makes decisions. But that view is incompatible with the confession that *God* is sovereign and that man lives his whole life—from the most significant decision to the least important—under the law of God (Matt. 22:37–40; 1 Cor. 10:31). Even the tiniest matter is included in the wide context of one's life and is never excluded as something "indifferent." This point we must grant to the Pietists. For that reason, I join them in drawing the conclusion that the term *adiaphora* is unsuitable. I defined *adiaphora* as things and actions that cannot be called either good or evil. But we cannot use the term *adiaphora* in referring either to "things" or to "actions." In our discussion of the Stoics, we observed that a mistaken view of God's creation underlies the notion of adiaphora. When all is said and done, man places himself autonomously above and beyond the creation and labels as "adiaphora" all sorts of things that God has created good. Scripture speaks differently. This is wonderfully illustrated in Romans 14:14, where Paul says that "there is nothing unclean of itself." Notice Paul's abstraction here. Nothing is unclean "of itself." But he doesn't end up with a defense of adiaphora. Paul does not characterize things viewed "in themselves" as neither good nor evil, but as *not unclean*. And he is convinced of that in the Lord Jesus, just as in another epistle he is convinced that every creature is good and not to be rejected as long as it is received with thanksgiving, for it is sanctified by the Word of God and by prayer (1 Tim. 4:4–5). For everyone who knows Christ, nothing in itself is unclean or neutral; rather, everything is good. The earth is the Lord's and all its fullness (1 Cor. 10:26; Matt. 28:18).

FREEDOM FROM AND FREEDOM FOR

It's good that we pause here for just a moment. In talking about adiaphora, we can easily slip into constructing a zone where neutral decisions are made, because we are not dealing with faith and with Christ when we make decisions in this zone all by ourselves. But this is an alien notion for those who confess that they belong, body and soul, in life and in death, to Jesus Christ. In other words, the Christian has surrendered himself lock, stock, and barrel to his Savior. What then does freedom mean? The answer points us to two aspects of Christian freedom (see my more extensive discussion in Douma 1992, 26–32).

In the first place, Christian freedom is freedom *from* various things. We are free from sin (Rom. 6:19), from the law as an oppressive yoke (Rom. 7:1–6), from those gods that in reality are no gods (Gal. 4:8). All such "masters" have no power over us any longer, for Jesus Christ has delivered us from every form of slavery. Paul vigorously warns against all who would put Christians under a yoke, so that they lose their freedom. "Stand fast therefore in the liberty by which Christ has made us free, and do not be entangled again with a yoke of bondage" (Gal. 5:1). So too during the course of church history, believers have been regularly warned against various forms of bondage, regardless of whether the threat came from the Roman Catholic side or the Protestant side. Pietism, too, in some of its expressions, threatened Christian liberty. We observed that earlier. Anybody who cannot celebrate a joyful feast and who denies play to his children, because he and those around him must always be occupied with "spiritual things," endangers liberty. Instead of being free *from* every human yoke, people become enslaved again *under* a yoke of various rules that put life in a straitjacket.

But freedom *from* every human yoke is only one side of Christian liberty. The other side is that we are free *for* Jesus Christ. Freedom from legalism, from foreign gods, from well-intentioned but nonetheless narrow-minded opinions about festive celebration and enjoying a delicious meal, is apparently at the same time the freedom *for* something and someone else. It is the freedom henceforth to serve God and our neighbor. If you can say, as Paul says of himself (1 Cor. 9:19), that you are free from all men, then in the same breath you must join Paul in adding that you make yourself a servant to all. The second is the flip side of the first.

This is very relevant to the matter of adiaphora. When the Pietists put life in a straitjacket, they obscure that feature of Christian liberty known as freedom *from.* But when they reject the concept of adiaphora because all our life is Christ's domain and *no neutral zone exists,* they are absolutely right. The only problem is that they give the wrong content to that freedom, because they have no eye for the immensely wide terrain in which the Christian may make his own decisions in the maturity bestowed upon him by Christ. Armed with this knowledge, we are now ready to stipulate our own answer to the question of adiaphora.

DON'T RESTRICT IT TO LEISURE

We enjoy a large measure of latitude in our conduct, although it is always tied to our freedom before Christ. What is remarkable is how large this arena of freedom really is. We should not restrict that arena to the field of leisure activities, for we enjoy that latitude beyond that domain as well. We enjoy it not only when we play, but also when we make far-reaching decisions. Let me mention a couple of them.

It is an important decision in one's life whether to marry or not. Anybody who stays unmarried, even though he or she has the opportunity to marry, must be able to give an account before God. So too must the one who marries. But in neither case can we find in Scripture concrete, personal instruction that settles the matter. The same is true regarding the choice of one's life partner. "He who finds a wife finds a good thing, and obtains favor from the LORD," we read in Proverbs 18:22. But that wife must surely be sought by the man (young fellow) himself. In that search, he will need to keep in mind several general guidelines given in Scripture. He will know that this searching must include praying. Clearly this is no adiaphoron, but just as clearly it is a matter of freedom. We do not receive from God a communication that we must marry one particular woman.

The same is true of our career. Nurture and education can steer us in a certain direction, but in many cases there is also a wide area of freedom, where it comes down to our own choice. That choice can be quite foundational and can determine the course of our entire life. The latitude we experience in freedom before Christ is definitely not limited to matters on the fringe of our life.

It would be best to abandon the term *adiaphora*. We should not abandon the truth that people defend when using it, however: Christian liberty—a liberty that puts us in the service of Christ—gives us all manner of latitude. We employ this freedom in making very fundamental decisions, not simply in the arena of recreation.

THE PERMISSIBLE

Friedrich Schleiermacher (1768–1834) did not want to speak of adiaphora, but rather of the permissible. However, he did not think that this term belonged in the science of ethics; rather, it belonged to jurisprudence. A judge can hardly punish everything that is ethically wrong.

For example, if I spitefully throw my expensive watch on the cement and break it, that is ethically reprehensible, but the judge will not fine me for doing it. Various actions belong to our private life, to the arena of our thoughts and imagination, which the judge cannot touch. Both in his jurisprudence and in society itself, the judge encounters many imperfections that he may well find reprehensible, but not thereby juridically punishable.

In my opinion, we can nevertheless use the term *permissible* in ethics. But it applies then to matters about which we do not agree, matters about which we cannot use the Scriptures to condemn others. Someone may well be convinced that his own conduct is God's will. But that does not always give him the right to condemn another who doesn't see it the same way.

The Dutch theologian K. Schilder discussed such matters and was willing to use the term *adiaphora,* especially with an eye to relationships within the church. Strictly speaking, according to Schilder, adiaphora don't exist if we relate all things to God and His law. But adiaphora do exist if we recall that human interpreters of God's Word often fall short. Due to that *lack of clarity,* different convictions arise among Christians, and one must not seek to impose one's views in these unclear matters on the other.

It seems better to me not to call these unclear matters "adiaphora." Rather, we could call them "permissible things." But we must remember that this phrase does not cover nearly everything relating to our mature freedom. For the characterization of "permissible" could indeed be seen as a very restrictive qualification of those innumerable decisions whereby a person may give shape to his creative freedom. Schilder was referring to situations in which we must unfortunately agree to disagree about our conduct. This involves, then, differences that we regret, without claiming a right to cut through the issue at stake and insist that the other person is acting contrary to Scripture. Thus, there are in reality—even in closely related church groups—differences that we wish were not there. But alongside these differences, where we bear with each other, there are other differences over which we rejoice. These latter have everything to do with our Christian liberty and our mature enjoyment of that freedom.

ONCE MORE: DISCERNING WHAT REALLY MATTERS

We are better off abandoning the term *adiaphora.* When it comes to enjoying our freedom, why would we choose so meager and negative a term? When you experience your freedom as genuinely Christian freedom, you never want to live any part of life as though good and evil played no role, as if you yourself were the boss. That kind of neutrality does not exist for the Christian. In every part of life, we are bound to Christ, and that is not in tension with our liberty.

This is found as well in Philippians 1:9–10, a passage we

encountered earlier. There Paul is asking in his prayer that our love may abound more and more in clear insight and in all discernment, in order that we may distinguish what is excellent. The Greek uses the word *diapheronta* for "what is excellent." In his lexicon, W. Bauer explains that the *diapheronta* are contrasted with the *adiaphora* (Bauer 2000, 239). Paul's word usage shows that a Christian isn't someone who automatically knows what he needs to know to make his decisions. Just like Paul, every believer can consult Scripture, but even then he doesn't always have the answer in hand. He needs to receive insight and discernment to be able to distinguish what is best. This need—as I have said earlier—is not his shame, but his honor. Nothing in his life is "indifferent," for his entire life lies under the claim of Christ. What is involved, Philippians 1:10–11 tells us, is being pure and undefiled for the day of Christ, filled with the righteousness that comes through Christ, to the glory and praise of God. That is the point, in career and in marriage, in work and in play, in the big and in the little things of life.

This doesn't make Christian living a burdensome enterprise that requires everything to be carefully reasoned out, without any spontaneity. Pietism (at least in certain forms) makes it hard for people "to relax and enjoy life in any other way than stealthily," says W. J. Aalders. Aalders refers to Kierkegaard, who offered such a pleasant portrait of the butcher "who simply does his work and lives in the joyful awareness of being in God's service" (Aalders 1947, 420).

Living life so gravely, and so strongly holding our opinions about everything, even when we are relaxing, has become unnecessary for those who want to live "in Christ." He has ransomed us so that we can live unencumbered.

Literature

Aalders, W. J. 1947. *Handboek der ethiek.* 2d ed. Amsterdam: Holland.

Bauer, W. 2000. A *Greek-English lexicon of the New Testament and other early Christian literature.* 3d ed. Revised and edited by F. W. Danker. Chicago: University of Chicago Press.

Douma, J. 1974. Zijn er adiaphora? In *Almanak fides quadrat intellectum.* Kampen: Zalsman.

Douma, J. 1992. *Christelijke levensstijl.* Kampen: Van den Berg.

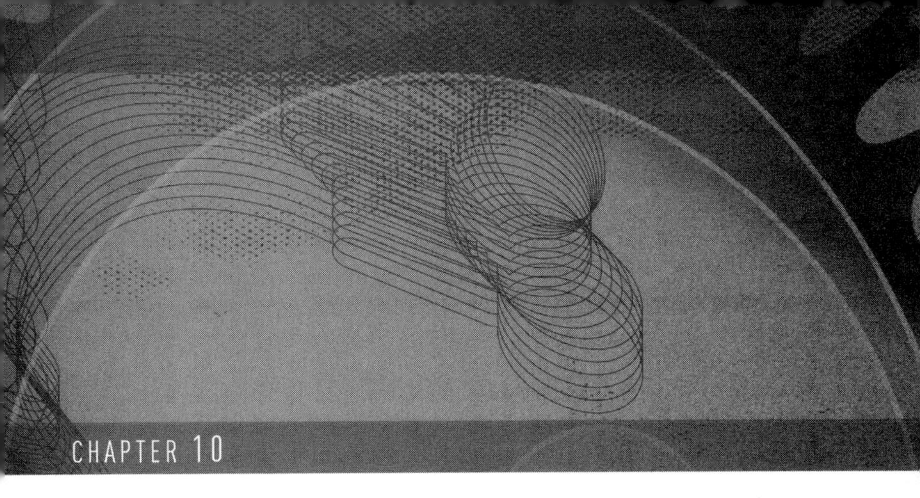

Is There a Conflict of Duties?

WHAT IS THE ISSUE?

Acting in freedom often means that we can go more than one way. Such is the case even when we are making important decisions in life—for example, when we choose a career. In many cases, choosing is not painful. But that is not so when our choices conflict. Then we must do either one thing or another. Then the prospect of choosing in freedom doesn't exist.

The painful nature of choosing can in certain situations be quite traumatic, since the question arises, If we do the one thing, are we not sinning by not doing the other? This question brings us to the theme of this chapter, namely, the collision of duties, or, to use the Latin phrase, *collisio officiorum.*

Several illustrations can clarify the issue. First, in a situation where pregnancy endangers the life of the mother, a physician must choose. If he chooses to save the life of the mother, then he must let the unborn child die. The reverse can also happen, but in both situations there is a victim. During World War II, many people offered their homes as refuge for those hiding from the Germans. Whenever the enemy knocked on the door to inquire whether the residents were hiding anybody, these people faced a choice: either tell the truth and thereby hand over to the enemy those who were hiding, or lie in order to rescue honorable countrymen from death. One more illustration: Two people stranded by a shipwreck have grabbed on to a board that is capable of holding only one of them. But which one? The one pushes the other off the board and saves himself at the cost of the other's life, or he lets go and surrenders to death.

The last illustration is a classic that appears in many older manuals of ethics. Such a situation occurred during World War II. The Reformed military chaplain Allard Pieron was captured by the Japanese. He was en route by ship to Japan. On the way, the ship was hit by a torpedo. Pieron made it into a lifeboat, but there was one person too many. In order to prevent everybody from losing their lives, one man had to sacrifice his life. Pieron volunteered and disappeared under the waves.

NOT ALL COMMANDMENTS ARE ABSOLUTE

Normally we tell the truth. Normally, however, we must also protect our neighbor's life. But what if both cannot be done, as in the situation I recalled from World War II? Both cannot be done at the same time, yet, taken separately, each is commanded by God. How do we solve this problem?

Let's begin with situations where we can make a clear choice, even though that choice may be difficult. Imagine a youngster whose parents demand that he profane God's name. For a believer, the matter is clear: the command of God supersedes that of man. We must obey God rather than men (Acts 4:19; 5:29). There is here a conflict of duties, but the choice is clear. *People* confront us with this conflict, not *God*. Only one choice can be made, namely, for God and against the parents. The two duties are completely unequal.

This illustration brings into view the real question of this chapter. That youngster must respect the third commandment, but the fifth commandment comes from God also, doesn't it? Why should he choose to honor the third and not the fifth commandment?

The answer is that not every commandment of God is an *absolute* commandment. An absolute commandment demands obedience irrespective of the concrete situation. The first and the third commandments of the Decalogue are such commandments. I can imagine no situation where people may honor another god or profane God's name. Joseph Fletcher thinks that the opposite is true. A person may formally abandon his faith in order to save the life of another, he says (Fletcher 1966, 72). Apparently the life of a person in need outweighs the honor to God.

The command to honor one's father and mother is not absolute. Whoever loves his father or mother more than Christ is not worthy of Him (Matt. 10:37). There are some circumstances in which one must renounce one's parents for the sake of Christ's name (Matt. 19:29). Evidently not every command in the Decalogue bears an absolute character.

This brings more sharply into view the issue of the conflict of duties. The real question is whether *God Himself* ever places contradictory duties before us. A conflict of duties can arise between what He demands of us and what people demand of us. But can we imagine a conflict of contradictory duties, both of which are pressed upon us by God?

If you make all the commands of the Decalogue absolute, to be obeyed in each and every circumstance, then you must conclude that God Himself gives us conflicting obligations. But then we must also agree that a dualism exists within God. He would be demanding from us at the same moment completely contradictory things.

TRAGEDY

Let's accept for the moment that a conflict of obligations is possible. Some people do in fact believe that God Himself can present us with such a conflict. That brings to mind the familiar theme of the Greek stage, namely, the theme of *tragedy*. The guilt in which man can become entangled is closely tied, for the ancient Greeks, to belief in fate and to polytheism. When one deity opposes another deity, the absolute demand of one can oppose the absolute demand of the other. Man is subjected to fate and is torn asunder by opposing duties.

Now a Christian does not accept that he can fall prey to the conflicting demands of various gods. Is it then correct to continue using the notion of tragedy? Some believe it is. Conflicting demands proceed, they say, not from conflicting gods in heaven above, but from discord in the world below.

This is maintained by S. J. Ridderbos in his book *Ethiek van het liefdegebod* (The ethics of the love command), whose subtitle is *Tragiek/compromis* (Tragedy/compromise). He argues that we should not remove the element of tragedy from the sphere of Christian faith. For then we would obscure the eschatological emphasis belonging to the Christian faith (Ridderbos 1975, 158).[1]

Now we can agree with Ridderbos that sin in our world has distorted many circumstances. The word "guilt" is never far away when we reflect on our relationship to God. But does this guilt bear a *tragic character*? Characteristic of tragedy is the fact that we have no influence upon it. Tragic guilt overtakes us unexpectedly and in fact without cause. But the kind of guilt that Scripture describes is attributable to us because we disobey God's commandments.

A chasm runs through the world and through our own lives, but not through the commands of God. We read that His commandments are not burdensome (1 John 5:3). Can we suppose, then, that by *His* commandments we are led into tragic situations?

MENDACIUM OFFICIOSUM

One particular resource in painful situations, where it can seem that God is placing us before conflicting obligations, is the command to love our neighbor. We know that all the

1 Dutch Reformed ethicist W. H. Velema also wants to be able to speak of a conflict of duties, since otherwise the tension resulting from the brokenness of life would be too quickly and too easily removed. See his article, "Ethiek tussen Eden en eschaton" (Ethics between Eden and the eschaton) in *Nuchtere noodzaak. Ethiek tussen navolging en compromis* (Harsh necessity: ethics between following [Christ] and compromise). In contrast to Ridderbos, Velema does avoid employing any notion of "the tragic."

commandments dealing with our relationships to other people are summarized in the command to love. Well, then, that is a useful resource for making the proper decision in conflict situations. It is impossible to obey a command of God and at the same time to flagrantly contradict the great love command.

For purposes of illustration, let's recall those noble patriots whose homes were searched to arrest those in hiding during World War II. To the enemy's question whether they were hiding anybody, these citizens could not say yes. They said no, although that was not the case. But they said no, not because they were careless about the ninth commandment, but in order to prevent those in hiding from becoming victims of the German enemy. Silence would not have helped, since silence would have said plenty! Employing answers or actions with misleading meanings would have helped even less, for such responses would have intended precisely the same thing as lying, namely, misleading the enemy.[2]

To rescue one's neighbor, it may be necessary to lie for the sake of love. We call such a lie a *mendacium officiosum*, a lie (*mendacium*) used in rendering service to another (*officium*).

2 Occasionally a distinction is made between *dissimulatio* (using words and phrases with double entendre to mislead someone) and *simulatio* (using actions to mislead, like pretending to be crazy, as David did before king Achish, 1 Sam. 21:13–15). We might also mention the *restrictio mentalis:* when a person uses words that, if they are taken literally, are untrue, but become true if taken with the addition of a mental reservation. One might say to an enemy, "We have no one hiding in our house," thinking (without saying it), "We have no one hiding in our house *for you to arrest.*" (For this and other distinctions, see Lee 1979, 71–77. In what follows, I have borrowed substantially from Lee's study.)

In perilous situations, lying can be the only means of rescuing others or ourselves.[3]

Should we not still say, however, that such lying conflicts with the ninth commandment, no matter how noble and necessary it may be to rescue those in hiding or rescue others? The ninth commandment forbids us to use false testimony against our neighbor. But one does precisely that against the neighbor standing at the door looking for people in hiding! Or was the German perhaps only an enemy and not our neighbor? We can reply that our enemy is also our neighbor. And situations may occur where we must step in to rescue even our most hostile enemy. But it can also happen that we are able only by means of lying to rescue one neighbor from the claws of the other neighbor. In that situation, it is clear what love, as the great command, requires of us. Anyone who respects that command cannot simultaneously sin against the ninth commandment.

We could also consider distinguishing between breaking a commandment and sinning against it. The priests who worked in the temple on the Sabbath broke the Sabbath without being guilty (Matt. 12:5). So it is possible to do one and not the other. Something that is impermissible in ordinary situations for people in general can be permitted and commanded for *particular* people in *particular* circumstances (Lee 1979, 122). The fifth commandment requires respect for parents, but situations can arise where children properly dis-

3 In classical ethics, the *mendacium officiosum* is distinguished from two other kinds of lying: the *mendacium perniciosum*, lying that injures the neighbor, and the *mendacium iocosum*, lying in jest, where truth and falsehood cannot be easily distinguished by the listener.

obey their parents. The sixth commandment forbids murder, but one who in self-defense saves his own life by killing an intruder does not sin against this commandment. The eighth commandment forbids stealing, but when someone steals a loaf of bread to avert starvation, that is again an emergency situation, so though he breaks the commandment, he does not sin against the commandment. Similarly, the ninth commandment is not intended absolutely, as if we may never employ lying. Scripture provides examples of lying in emergency situations, without condemning any one of those acts. Think of the narrative of the midwives in Egypt (Ex. 1:15–21) and of Rahab (Josh. 2; James 2:25–26), or recall still other stories like these (Judg. 3:15–23; 4:18–21; 5:24–30; 2 Sam. 17:19–20). With incorrect information, we can rescue our neighbor's life, just as with correct information (as in gossip, for example) we can seriously injure our neighbor. Formally, we may well be in line with the ninth commandment as we tell others all kinds of true statements, and yet by speaking such "truth" we can seriously transgress the command of love.

THE OTHER EXAMPLES

To summarize what I have been saying, I would observe that we can speak of a conflict of duties when the situation involves duties that people require of us, but not duties that God demands of us. People can demand the impossible from us by placing two or more conflicting duties before us, but God's commandment does not contain such a contradiction.

Let's look again at those illustrations I gave earlier in this chapter, examples I have not examined up to this point. Whenever a choice must be made between the life of a mother and that of an unborn child, that is a painful situation. Most often the life of the mother will be chosen rather than that of the child. But we could also imagine the alternative choice. A mother might sacrifice herself for her child. Suppose that the sixth commandment required absolute respect for every human life; then we would be dealing with tragedy in deciding between the life of the mother and the life of the child. No matter which choice we made, we would be sinning. But the sixth commandment does not have this absolute character. Therefore, the choice between the two possibilities, no matter how grievous, does not constitute a conflict of duties. God does not command the one and the other, leaving us morally torn asunder. He requires us to distinguish what is best. When we make a responsible decision, we do not sin against God's commandment.

Nor does the illustration of the two drowning men exhibit a conflict of duties. In that situation, a prohibition against suicide does not conflict with the requirement of self-denial. For whoever sacrifices his life for his neighbor in such a situation is not committing suicide. To talk of suicide here is to slide into abstraction. This is remarkably clear from what Pieron said when he prepared to step out of the lifeboat to sacrifice himself for the others: "I can die. I have a Savior who has bought me with His blood." One who says something like this is not planning suicide, but sacrificing himself for his neighbor's benefit. His is a free choice with no trace of the tragic, an example of loving one's neighbor.

We could provide more difficult illustrations of situations in which suicide is indeed relevant. What should a person do who, under the pressure of expert interrogation, could betray his friends? May he take his own life to save them? A Christian would recoil from doing so, mindful of Christ's word, "It will be given to you in that hour what you should speak" (Matt. 10:19). If someone had killed himself to spare his friends, we should be careful about condemning such a decision. But here too we need not speak of a conflict of duties.

CAREFULNESS

None of the illustrations I have been discussing is an everyday occurrence. Seldom are people faced, in connection with a complicated pregnancy, with choosing between the mother's life or the child's life. Fortunately, wartime situations with people in hiding, a shipwreck with the prospect of imminent drowning, and encountering torture do not occur in the lives of most people. Nevertheless, even in ordinary life conflicts occur. The emergency lie can suddenly become quite relevant when someone is terminally ill, but cannot (yet) deal with the truth of that reality. What should we do in such a situation? Many manuals of ethics tell about the seriously ill mother who asks to see her child, but who could well die at the news that her beloved child is dead. Should we then say, with Fichte, "If the woman die of the truth, then let her die" (as mentioned by Thielicke 1979, 520–21)? That is a harsh judgment. I would rather say, with W. H. Velema, that it cannot be God's intention that someone be destroyed by our speaking the truth (1973, 69).

However, less unusual situations arise where we withhold the truth from the terminally ill, either out of cowardice or laziness. Of these situations J. J. Buskes says, "Is the measure of a person's ability to bear the truth about his disease our standard for determining what we may and must say to him?

Even in ordinary life, if we care at all for each other, we tell each other this or that which we cannot bear. . . . Death is such a radical event that when we know a loved one is dying, we will not mislead him and thus deny him the opportunity to prepare for death" (1964, 127). Buskes also acknowledges that every rule has its exception. But the rule he identifies here is very important. We may never break the ninth commandment lightly. We must speak the truth, even when it is painful.

Clear insight and discernment are required here too. We must handle the truth with care. For this art we need the leading of God's Spirit. Growing in the truth also occurs as we maintain the ninth commandment in our lives. Dietrich Bonhoeffer provides a beautiful example of this (1955, 367). A pupil was asked by his teacher in front of the class whether it was true that his father often came home drunk. It was true, but the child denied it. The teacher's question created a situation with which the child could not cope. To Bonhoeffer's example, B. M. Lee adds the observation that, had the child been older and more mature, he could have replied, "May I talk with you about this alone during recess?" (1979, 151–52).

Literature

Bonhoeffer, D. 1955. *Ethics.* Edited by Eberhard Bethge. New York: Macmillan.

Buskes, J. J. 1964. *Waarheid en leugen aan het ziekbed.* 3d ed. Baarn: Ten Have.

Fletcher, J. 1966. *Situation ethics.* Philadelphia: Westminster Press.

Lee, B. M. 1979. *Mendacium officiosum.* Groningen: De Vuurbaak.

Ridderbos, S. J. 1975. *Ethiek van het liefdegebod.* Kampen: Kok.

Thielicke, Helmut. 1979. *Theological ethics.* Vol. 1, *Foundations.* Edited by William H. Lazareth. Philadelphia: Fortress.

Velema, W. H. 1973. *Leer er mee te leven*. Kampen: Kok.

Velema, W. H. 1997. Ethiek tussen Eden en eschaton. In *Nuchtere noodzaak. Ethiek tussen navolging en compromis: opstellen aangeboden aan prof. dr J. Douma*, edited by J. H. F. Schaeffer, J. H. Smit, and Th. Tromp. Kampen: Kok.

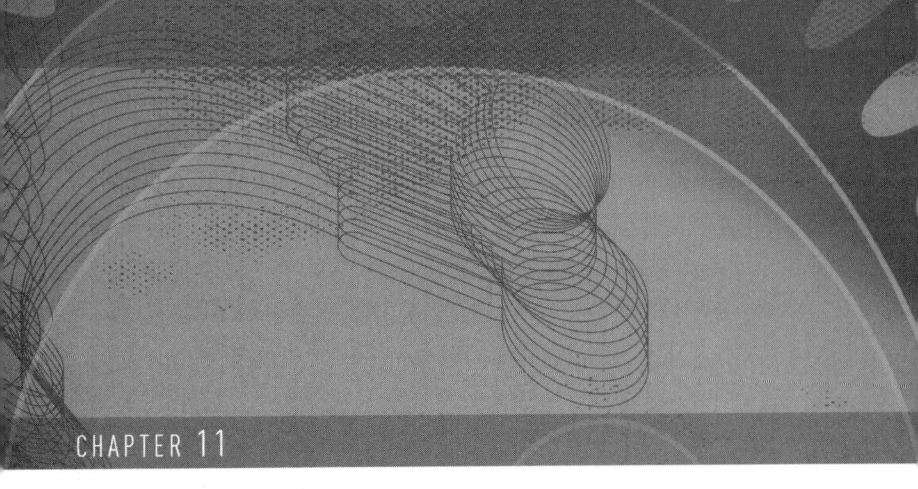

Compromise

ACCEPTING LESS THAN WE WOULD LIKE

The subject now under discussion lies close to the themes of adiaphora and conflict of duties. Let me briefly summarize what we have been saying.

In every area of life, we are dealing with the command of God. For that reason, it seems to me to be inappropriate to speak of areas where our decisions would supposedly bear the character of adiaphora. It is certainly true that we may decide about many matters without being under constraint; but while enjoying such liberty, we must constantly seek God's will. In our Christian liberty, we realize that we are always bound to Christ. Therefore, no neutral zones exist, areas where we could go our own way without thought of Christ.

Next, we discussed the issue of conflict of duties. Does God sometimes make obeying His commands difficult for us because He places us before two simultaneously conflicting obligations? We observed that even though people fall short in many things and stand guilty before God, they never land in situations where they *must* sin on account of a conflict of duties that *God Himself* has supposedly put before them.

In this chapter, a third important issue arises. Even when we have a clear understanding of God's command, it is not always possible to enforce it among people. This is true not only because we ourselves fall far short in our own obedience, but also because others prevent us from obeying God's command. It is this last reason that I am concerned with now. To what extent must we factor into our moral awareness those other people who are hindering what we believe to be necessary and salutary? And to what extent should we adapt our conduct to their expectations? We are dealing here with the issue of *compromise*.

The word *compromise* comes from the Latin word *compromittere*, meaning "to reach a settlement, to reach an agreement." I define a compromise as *the necessary acceptance of less than what one may and must strive for on the basis of God's command.*

SOME EXAMPLES

A few examples will serve to illustrate this definition.

Scripture solemnly warns us against the evil of divorce. Yet many people are unfaithful and get divorced. May a civil government, which must deal with the consequences of that conduct, develop a policy that legalizes divorce?

Scripture clearly teaches, "You shall not murder." We are convinced that this includes the duty of protecting unborn children. But suppose many women demand the right to abortion and that a large part of the population wants to expand by legislation the opportunities for abortion. May a Christian cooperate with that?

Scripture teaches that we must love our neighbor. We deduce from this that discrimination is a violation of this command. If Arab countries, for anti-Semitic reasons, request proof from their Western business partners that they are not Jews, may we approve such conduct so that business may flow unimpeded? May a church's governing body provide a certificate of baptism for that purpose?

During World War II, the Dutch had to resist German National Socialism. But during those years, what was a town mayor supposed to do? If he conceded much in order to remain in office, he could still provide significant help to loyal countrymen. Should he have refused to continue as town mayor?

CHARACTERISTICS OF GENUINE ETHICAL COMPROMISE

Before going any further—quite apart from formulating answers in response to these examples—we need to recognize that compromise is unavoidable as long as we are living in this broken world. We encounter compromise in Scripture. Moses permitted divorce on account of the "hardness of heart" among the Israelites, even though divorce conflicted with what God had declared when He created man and woman (Deut. 24:1–4; Matt. 19:3–9). Paul forbade contact with sexually immoral people who had been cut off from the church, but not with the sexually immoral in the world in general, or with covetous people, thieves, or idolaters. For, he explained, then we would have to leave the world (1 Cor. 5:9–13). There are such people around us, and the Christian has to deal with them.

In this mixed world, where the powerful forces of evil hold so much sway, Christians are often unable to give shape to the gospel in public life. I should add immediately that this is true also within the church, unfortunately. Recall the hardness of heart to which Jesus referred. Such an attitude surfaced in Israel, the people of God. Recall the definition of compromise I gave earlier. Don't we often have to be satisfied *in the church* with less than what should be pursued on the basis of God's command? We are referring to things like quarrels among church members and minor differences between various church groups. Personal grievances between church members are occasionally "resolved" by sweeping them under the rug, without anybody ever confessing guilt for injuring relationships. That too is a compromise. In order to prevent a bad situation from becoming worse, a matter is closed to further debate without anybody having to walk the royal road of expressing remorse and acknowledging guilt. Church denominations that are unified in fundamental matters should unite formally in order to express the unity that Jesus Himself prayed for (John 17:20–21). Sadly, many denominations find it safer to continue living independently alongside each other than to accept the challenges involved in every unification effort. This reality, too, possesses an element of compromise.

What, then, are the characteristic features of *acceptable* compromise? First, we must have a *conflict between competing interests.* Not everything called compromise meets the ethical definition of that term. You might call the modern family automobile a compromise between the demands of speed and comfort. But that is not a conflict in the ethical sense of the word. Nor is the problem of time management for a preacher who needs time for study, pastoral work, his own family, and the like. The difficulties involved in proper time management don't bear the ethical weight we usually associate with a conflict.

A genuine ethical conflict isn't simply about an opinion, but about a weighty conviction. A conviction is something you stand on, something foundational that you don't easily surrender (Van den Bergh 1965, 3). This is why, in my Christian ethics, I refer in my definition of compromise to God's command. On various issues and opinions, people can reach agreement, possibly even painfully so, without their agreement having the seriousness of a compromise in the sense that I have described.

Secondly, the element of *necessity* must be present. A genuine compromise offers no way of escape. The injury suffered by rejecting the compromise must be greater than that occasioned by accepting it. William Perkins warns against going for the best if in the process we would lose the second best. It is better to be satisfied with the second best than to chase what ultimately lies beyond our reach. He refers to the wise counsel of the Preacher, "Do not be overly righteous" (Eccl. 7:16). Among the examples he then provides is that of divorce in Israel. By permitting divorce, God restrained the evil that otherwise could not be fought. God gave the law of the divorce certificate, not to allow people to commit sin without restraint, nor to remove sin entirely, but to moderate evil. In a situation involving compromise, we must always preserve our faith and a good conscience, but Perkins argues that it may be necessary to make temporary concessions, just as we do when navigating a river. Often swimming against the current is impossible.

Thirdly, in genuine compromise the element of *forbearance* plays a role. God is patient with this world, and therefore our attitude should reflect His. We have already become acquainted with the Latin proverb *Fiat iustitia, pereat mundus*: "Justice must have its way, even if the world perishes" (see chap. 2). Surely this is no Christian proverb, since it testifies to a zeal without understanding. It reminds us of Jonah, who wanted to see Nineveh destroyed (Jonah 4:1–3), quite unlike Jonah's God, who spared Nineveh, and who showed and still shows so much patience to this godless world (Rom. 2:4; 9:22; 2 Peter 3:9). Uncompromising radicalism dreams of a new world and forgets that Christians must still exercise patience with a love that is forbearing (1 Cor. 13:4).

Fourthly, no compromise exists apart from *personal suffering* because of it. All ethical compromise is unfortunate (Velema 1968, 159–62). But compromise is never a definitive solution. Although we must accept compromise, we may not be resigned to compromise. We may not easily shrug off the sense that we are unable to attain anything more than what the compromise made possible. We cannot attain the maximum, but we should not be satisfied with the minimum. Therefore, we should continue our efforts at forming a society that listens better to God's command than it now does.

LIMITS

Naturally, there are limits to compromise. Often we must be satisfied with less than what we may and must pursue on the basis of God's command. But less is always more than nothing. Any Christian who merely goes with the flow and fears the opposition of the majority is not a good defender of God's command. In fact, such a Christian is not reaching genuine compromises at all, but merely suffering defeats.

For there are boundaries that may not be trespassed. We may not agree to any compromise that would curtail the unrestrained profession of our faith. We must obey God rather than men (Acts 5:29). Perhaps a situation may arise where we might be able to rescue our own life or that of another by obeying men rather than God. But no matter how worthy of protection a human life may be, preserving that life cannot sacrifice obedience to God's command.

We certainly may not agree to a compromise that constitutes a license for killing our neighbor. Such is the case when we approve the legalization of abortion on demand. Here we may not leave the door ajar at all. A compromise with regard to abortion on demand always means that we are taking upon ourselves responsibility for killing unborn children. The argument that abortion on demand will still be legalized even if we oppose it, and that we could therefore better work to limit its impact, appears invalid to me. In a situation involving life and death, we may not be selective, abandoning some in order to rescue others.

But cooperating with efforts to change *existing* abortion policies is an altogether different matter. We should seize every improvement that can lead to fewer victims, even though we will be unable to totally reverse pro-abortion legislation.

I would pause here to point out the difference between pro-abortion legislation and divorce legislation. In order to restrain human lawlessness, the government must intervene, limiting the evil of divorce as much as possible by means of legislation. But with a law permitting abortion on demand, the government permits killing (unborn) human beings. Ending a marriage is something else than ending a life. Legislative intervention with regard to divorce is something else than legislative intervention that opens up the possibility of snuffing out the life of defenseless human beings.

Another limit of acceptable compromise is reached when we observe that we would be going backward instead of forward—that is, we would be unable to move in a better direction. Here I am thinking of the situation of the town mayor during the German occupation of the Netherlands. You may well have noble intentions of helping loyal countrymen by remaining in an office whose function has become dubious, but if you must collaborate with the enemy, the question arises whether you are doing more evil than good. Good is quickly overgrown by evil.

Sometimes we must dare to say no, even if there are comparable circumstances in which we might say yes. Recall the example of needing to prove that someone is not Jewish. People discriminate in any number of ways. To attack every form of discrimination at once is to attempt the impossible. But that means it may be necessary to send a *signal* by denouncing the evil of discrimination in particular situations. Such a signal would be sent by church bodies and other groups who refuse to furnish proof to satisfy anti-Semitic sentiments.

DOES COMPROMISE RENDER ONE GUILTY?

Some people believe that every compromise renders us guilty. Now, that is true in many cases, when we inadequately defend the honor of God and the welfare of our neighbor. But does each and every compromise render us guilty? If that is the case, then we should dare to accuse Moses of sinning when he declared the certificate of divorce to be permissible.

But he acted in the service of God. If God permits something, and we follow in His steps, are we then sinning?

There is a difference between something being harmful and something being sinful. Undoubtedly every compromise involves harm. After all, we must settle for less than what we would prefer on the basis of God's command. That involves harm. We should feel bad that a compromise is necessary. Together with others, we stand guilty for things going so badly in the world. But this does not yet mean that each compromise also compromises us. As long as God has a job for us to do in this world, there will be Josephs and Daniels who, in an environment hostile toward God, without overreaching their position, will have to accept less than they desire. And they will do so with all the resulting harm for that environment and for themselves. But are they then living in a compromising fashion that we should call sinful?

Indeed, some compromises cannot be reached without guilt. What Naaman said is striking. After his healing, he declared that he would offer no burnt offering or sacrifice to any god other than the Lord. But he returned to his pagan land with the god Rimmon. There, when he would have to provide physical assistance to the king of Syria in the temple of Rimmon, he would also have to bow before this god! For that, he asked Elisha for the Lord's forgiveness (2 Kings 5:18–19). Elisha answered, "Go in peace." Interpretations of these words vary. Some understand that Elisha allowed the request, and as God's spokesman guaranteed Naaman the requested forgiveness. For the sake of serving the God of Israel, Naaman did not need to jeopardize his position in the palace and his own life. Others judge this with more reservation. Elisha would not have given approval, but would have commended Naaman to the further leading of the Lord and to His grace. I hold to the first view. “Go in peace” is not, in my opinion, an answer in which Elisha refused to commit himself. Elisha raised no objection to what Naaman wanted; he did not reply with a “Yes, but . . .” Why, then, would we say that here?

Literature

Van den Bergh, R. 1965. *Het compromis*. Publikatie Nederlands Gesprek Centrum. Kampen: Kok.

Velema, W. H. 1968. Grenzen en gestalten van het compromis. *Theologia reformata* 11:147–62.

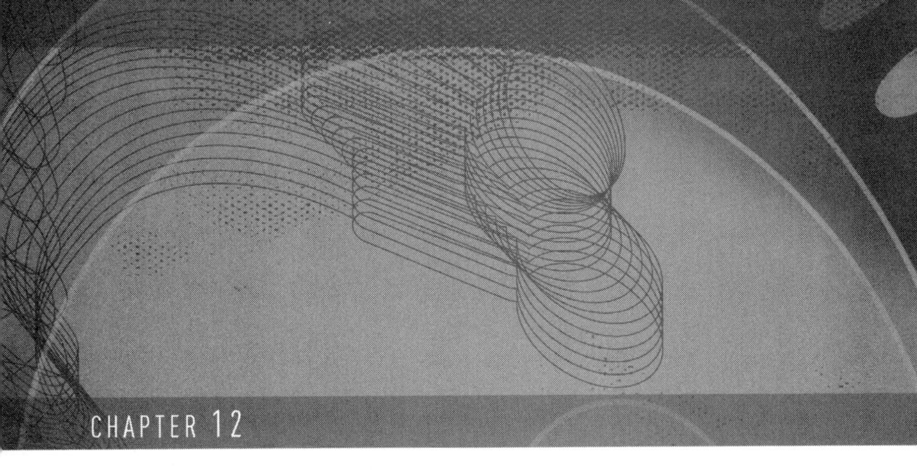

Casuistry

FROM THE GENERAL TO THE SPECIFIC

In more than one chapter, we have seen how valuable Christian liberty is as an element of responsible conduct. The Christian acknowledges God's commandments that directly point out the way he is to walk in many situations, but he also encounters situations where he has no direct answer. In chapter 9, we asked, Are there adiaphora? There we observed that very deep-rooted decisions for directing our lives may and must be reached very personally.

Naturally, we can learn a lot from one another. Often we like to get advice from others before we make a decision. Perhaps others have better insight regarding God's command in our circumstances. The same applies to evaluating the circumstances of our situation. Are we taking all the factors into consideration? How much weight should we give to one, and how much to another?

Here is an example: The sixth commandment forbids us to kill. But what does this commandment have to do with euthanasia? In a situation where a comatose patient can be kept alive only with artificial medical procedures, are we in conflict with the sixth commandment if we pull the plug and allow him to die? May a person who knows that he is going to die from a terminal disease refuse an operation that might extend his life a little bit?

In such situations, it is understandable that we ask advice from each other. That does not infringe upon our freedom, but enables us to use our freedom properly, when we are equipped by others with a better knowledge of the issues.

This subject leads us, then, to the theme of casuistry. The term *casuistry* comes from the Latin word *casus*, which means "case." Casuistry can be described as the *study of cases teaching us how we should apply general rules to specific cases*.

People have often spoken of *casus conscientiae*, or cases of conscience. They are referring to the issue of how we, with a good conscience, should act in various cases where we have no specific command from God.

CASUISTRY'S BAD NAME

Suppose that we opt for a situational ethic. Such an ethic would have no room for casuistry. This is because every situational ethic denies the existence of any general rule that is valid for everyone, as we saw in chapter 7. When situational ethicists do speak of a command, it is the command of love. As long as you act lovingly, you may do what you want. What you should do depends on the situation. Apart from the situation, there are no fixed rules and norms. The command does not *enter* the situation, we saw, but must *arise within* the situation. Situations are viewed as unique, and none is a "case" that can be placed alongside other cases. Situation ethics frustrates all casuistry that assumes you can fix beforehand how you should act in a particular situation. This is evident in the situation ethics of Joseph Fletcher, which he himself characterizes as neo-casuistic (Fletcher 1966, 148).

But some ethicists who would never defend situation ethics of any kind nevertheless object to casuistry. That is understandable, for in its long history, casuistry has shown its dark side rather frequently. In the past, casuistry has woven an entire tapestry of precepts and prohibitions, a network leaving no room for personal freedom and responsibility toward God and neighbor. Recall the Pharisees, with their 613 commands and prohibitions (apparently corresponding to the 613 Hebrew letters used in the Ten Commandments). Recall as well the Roman Catholic moral theologians whose casuistry, packaged in part in the church's confessional manuals, consisted of ranking, analyzing, and evaluating sins down to the smallest detail.

For no fewer than two hundred years (the seventeenth and eighteenth centuries), Roman Catholic moral theology revolved around the problem of probabilism in casuistry. It is instructive to look briefly at the battleground of moral theology in those days. Probabilism was one of several systems competing for preeminence at that time. Every system wanted to solve the conflict between law and freedom. How far may someone go in his freedom of action if there is no clear demand of the law? (What follows is based on Gallagher 1974, 139ff.).

Suppose that someone must choose between actions A and B. Action A is clearly morally good, while the moral quality of action B is doubtful. How did various ethical systems choose between them?

The system known as *tutiorism* taught that you should choose the safest path, and so should choose action A.

The system called *probabiliorism* taught that you might equally well choose action B, provided that it is more likely to be morally good than morally bad.

The system known as *probabilism* taught that you might choose action B if any probability existed that it might be called good, even though it was probably morally wrong. If you could supply the names of a few writers who defended action B, then you were justified in taking that action.

The system called *laxism* went to the limit. Action B could be taken if any renowned author said that it was good. However, laxism was openly condemned by the church.

Moreover, various exceptions were made to prevent the application of probabilism from causing serious moral injuries. When matters like the valid administration of the sacraments, the endangering of a person's salvation, the injury of one's neighbor, or church fellowship were involved, a sure, rather than an unsure, path had to be taken. Action A was then to be chosen rather than action B. Imagine the case of a hunter who sees something moving in the trees. He could suppose that he was seeing a deer moving. But suppose there was a remote chance that what he saw moving among the trees was a person! In that case, he should choose the sure, rather than the unsure, and not shoot.

It is no wonder that opposition arose to every form of extensively developed casuistry. A man by the name of Antonius Diana, in his *Resolutiones morales*, dealt with more than twenty thousand cases of conscience! Among the best-known opponents of casuistry was Blaise Pascal (1623–62), who wrote *Lettres provinciales* against the Jesuits.

So casuistry can degenerate into precept upon precept and rule upon rule. Or, a system of casuistry can file down the sharp edges of the obedience we owe to God. Both can occur together, as we see in the ethics of the Pharisees, which Jesus sharply condemned. They tithed mint, dill, and cummin (rather insignificant herbs), while they neglected the weightiest matters of the law, such as justice, mercy, and faithfulness. They strained out the gnat, but swallowed the camel (Matt. 23:23–24). This is how casuistry gets a bad name.

PROTESTANT CASUISTRY

Naturally, the Reformation criticized various precepts and prohibitions that the Roman Catholic Church had put in place during the preceding centuries. Did this mean that the churches of the Reformation denied a place for casuistry? No, for both the Lutherans and the Reformed soon developed their own casuistry. Can we conclude from this that we must be cautious in rejecting casuistry as such?

Protestant writers dealing with ethical matters attempted to avoid the mistakes of Roman Catholic casuistry. I am thinking at this point of theologians like William Perkins (1558–1602), William Ames (1576–1633), and Gisbertus Voetius (1589–1676). They wrote extensive treatises of casuistry, bearing a number of remarkable features.

1. They viewed Scripture as the only authority for faith and morals. Other authorities had little or no authority at all.

2. They emphasized the general principles of morality and provided selected cases as examples, but left the responsibility for precise application to individual believers.

3. They made casuistry a popular science accessible to

everybody, and thus not only to the priest-confessor. Each believer could be, as it were, his or her own priest-confessor.

4. They disregarded every distinction between venial and mortal sins, which operated in Roman Catholic teaching. In principle, every sin is mortal, although sins do indeed differ in degree. This rejection of a distinction between venial and mortal sins dismantled the foundation underlying the Latin tradition of casuistry.

5. They opposed probabilism with all their might. Rather, we find in Voetius, Ames, and others a clear link to tutiorism (choosing the safest path).[1]

ONCE MORE: THE OBJECTIONS

Casuistry can obviously be practiced in a way different from that of the Pharisees and the Roman Catholic Church. But can it be practiced in such a way that it becomes fully acceptable? Permit me to mention a number of objections advanced even against better forms of casuistry.

Casuistry is said to lead to a forceful splintering of God's command. When Calvin speaks of splitting sins into the branches, twigs, and leaves of a tree (*Institutes* 3.4.17; see also 4.10), does this not characterize every form of casuistry? Does

1 For these five features see Sprunger (1972, 164) and Beardslee (1965, 278, note 22). For tutiorism in Voetius and others, see Voetius (1659, 32). Whether choosing the safest path was always choosing the best path is open to question. Often this choosing contained a dose of conservatism. New paths may well be better, but many shrink from embarking upon them because that which is new involves risks and we really want everybody moving together. Think of issues like a new church songbook or a new Bible translation!

not casuistry always lead to an ethical atomism? Is the unity of God's command, especially the comprehensive command of love, kept in view when everything is divided up into little segments? Do we still see the forest for the trees? Does not the Martha of busy casuistry almost patently yearn for the Mary of the one thing needful?

Further, does not casuistry easily assume a negative and legalistic character? Casuistry is always untangling, in ever refining detail, everything that is impermissible. Fear of crossing the line can become an obsession. Such a practice obscures the gospel of our freedom in Christ. Moreover, people are made to depend on experts who think they know precisely what may and may not be done.

Finally, does not casuistry ignore the uniqueness of the concrete situation in which we must again and again make our decisions?

These objections are worthy of full consideration. Casuistry always presents dangers lurking on every side. But are the objections that I have summarized really convincing? I think not. For we can assemble counterarguments to each of these objections.

To the first we reply that *specializing* the command of God is different than *splintering* it. After giving us the Ten Commandments in Exodus 20 and Deuteronomy 5, Scripture gives us many particularizations introduced with the phrase, "Whenever this or that happens, then . . ." These are casuistic prescriptions, introduced with the Hebrew words *ki* or *im,* distinct from the so-called apodictic prescriptions, which take the categorical form "thou shalt," "he shall," "a person shall," or "they shall." In a good form of casuistry, particularization does not descend to the details of various individual situations, but deals with *types* of situations and is therefore more general in character than it might appear at first glance.

To the second objection we reply that while casuistry can lead to legalism, it can also render a service. It sounds heroic, writes W. J. Aalders, to say to someone, "Follow your conscience," but that can be cruel (quoted in De Vos 1961, 224). In the church, we do not stand alone, so in our effort to discern what is excellent we may expect the assistance of others.

To the third objection we observe that situations in life are seldom so unique that they cannot be compared with other situations. The problems of daily living are recognizable to many. In our day-to-day living, things are rarely one of a kind, and our decisions are seldom unique. We must guard against standardized, ready-to-wear approaches in casuistry. But we may also soberly observe that more people sport ready-to-wear clothes than wear custom-tailored garments. Our Christian liberty does not obviate the fact that as members of the body of Christ we display a strikingly similar lifestyle.

MORAL COUNSEL

The term *casuistry* does not have a good sound to it. If we want to use another term, we might consider the phrase *moral counsel*. For that is what good casuistry is really all about. By providing such counsel, we are not restraining our neighbor's life, but contributing to its proper development. Such counsel does not minimize our personal responsibility, as so often argued, but is precisely what activates it. I need to know how I must act in various situations that occur or can occur in my life. Why then would I refuse to accept the good counsel of others?

Only the person who thinks that he must and can walk life's path by himself would refuse such counsel. But someone who realizes that there are many problems that he faces or will face in common with others, will be happy that he does not stand alone, but in the fellowship of the church.

Together we have to reach personal maturity, the measure of the wisdom of the fullness of Christ (Eph. 4:12–13). Moral counsel serves that goal. We take in hand the information that we need to arrive at a personal decision that we ourselves—with personal responsibility, and thus with a knowledge of the issues—must make.

This moral counsel has always been offered in the church. I am thinking of the moral advice of men like Ambrose and Augustine. I think of the many letters that Calvin sent to render advice regarding various questions, such as marriage.

The manuals of casuistry written in former days have become unusable. We need not exert ourselves today to prepare answers for every real or imaginable "case." We do not need an elaborate casuistry. But there are still cases, and often new cases, about which we talk together and for which we can find support in the counsel that others give us.

We may not play off the *case* against the *situation*, as if the former makes ethics into something impersonal and the latter really shows us how unique our life is. Innumerable situations are very ordinary, and even if some are extraordinary, they are usually not so special that only the person involved is dealing with them. Thousands of people face similar situations, cases that make general advice possible. This generalizing does not minimize what is special about each human life. Each person will acknowledge God's special leading in his or her personal life. But that should not detract from recognizing another reality, namely, that we stand together under the same commandments of God, and that we have to make the same decisions in our own special situations.[2]

Literature

Beardslee, John W., ed. 1965. *Reformed dogmatics.* New York: Oxford University Press.

De Vos, H. 1961. Casuïstiek. *Kerk en theologie* 12:217–32.

Fletcher, Joseph. 1966. *Situation ethics.* Philadelphia: Westminster Press.

Gallagher, J. 1974. Probabilism and possible abortifacients. In *Death before birth,* edited by E. J. Kremer and A. A. Synan. Toronto: Griffin House.

Kloosterman, Nelson D. 1997. Casuistry as ministerial ethics. *Nuchtere noodzaak. Ethiek tussen navolging en compromis: opstellen aangeboden aan prof. dr J. Douma,* edited by J. H. F. Schaeffer, J. H. Smit, and Th. Tromp. Kampen: Kok.

Sprunger, K. L. 1972. *The learned doctor William Ames.* Chicago: University of Illinois Press.

Voetius, Gisbertus. 1659. *Disputationes selectae.* Utrecht.

2 N. D. Kloosterman identifies the analogous character of moral situations: "Continuity within history (including every moral situation) makes the use of analogy *possible*. Discontinuity within history (including every moral situation) makes the use of analogy *necessary*" (Kloosterman 1997, 111).

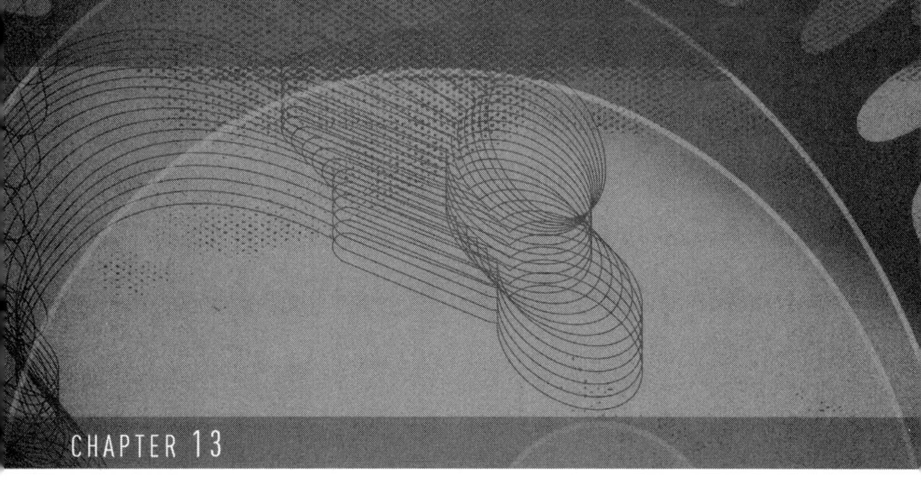

Spirituality

SPIRITUALITY AND ETHICS

At the conclusion of this introduction to Christian ethics, I return to my definition of Christian ethics. I have described Christian ethics as reflection on moral conduct from the perspective offered to us in Holy Scripture (see chap. 2). In chapter 3, this definition led us to observe that Christian ethics occupies a limited arena. Morality is the arena of interpersonal conduct. Ethics reflects on that, and not, for example, on the direct relationship between man and God as that is experienced in prayer, Bible study, meditation, church life, and public worship. These latter subjects are not treated extensively in Christian ethics.

Nevertheless, such themes are very significant for Christian ethics, for they involve our *spirituality*. By "spirituality," I understand *the exercise of, and reflection upon, our fellowship with the triune God.*

Anybody can understand that *Christian* ethics has a lot to do with spirituality. The relationship between ethics and spirituality is obvious when we consider the Ten Commandments, with its two tables—the first dealing with our relation to God, and the second with our relation to our neighbor. What would become of Christian ethics if we treated the second table apart from the first? And what would our moral conduct be worth as Christian conduct if it did not drink from the fountain of prayer, Bible study, meditation, church life, and public worship?

In chapter 3, I mentioned that W. Geesink identified the relationship between people as moral, and that between people and God as religious or sacred. This is how he limited the arena of ethics. But along with his ethics, Geesink devoted attention, even as his Reformed predecessors had, to what I here have called spirituality. How did he do that? By calling spirituality a *means for assisting* in the formation of human character or virtue (Geesink 1931, 2:243–66). Within ethics, attention to human virtue is indispensable, as we have observed. Virtue is concerned, not so much with what a person *does*, as with who a person *is* (chap. 2). So then, who are we? We are children of God, redeemed by Christ and led by the Holy Spirit. From the fountain of this *being*, our *doing* is supplied. I would call spirituality—our concourse with the triune God—the nutritional supply for our moral conduct and for our ethical reflection.

AN ANCIENT SUBJECT: ASCETICS

In the past, the study of theology included a subject that has disappeared from the curriculum for ministerial training. What I am calling spirituality was formerly called ascetics. Gisbertus Voetius, for example, not only taught *theologia moralis* or *casuistica*, in which he treated various ethical questions in terms of the Ten Commandments, but in addition gave instruction in *theologia ascetica*. Central to this subject was the discussion of prayer. Whereas he used as the basis for teaching casuistry the Heidelberg Catechism, Lord's Days 32–44 (dealing with the Decalogue), Lord's Days 45–52 (dealing with the Lord's Prayer) formed the basis for his teaching of ascetics. In this way, the entire life of gratitude, which we are obligated to live unto God (Lord's Days 32–52), received attention in the theological instruction of ethics and spirituality.

But the subject of ascetics disappeared from theological instruction, at least among the theological institutions in the Netherlands. In the early part of the twentieth century, Abraham Kuyper (1837–1920) still insisted that attention should be given to both parts, casuistics and ascetics (Kuyper 1909, 415–35), but in the subsequent years of the century not much came of it. There are more than enough ethical questions to discuss, and to that extent we could say that the line of casuistics has continued. But ascetics has disappeared from view.

This is not to say that theologians pay no attention to prayer and other means of maintaining our relationship with God. I am only signaling the fact that prayer has virtually disappeared from the field of *ethics*, and that this is striking in light of the history of Christian ethics.

The term *ascetics* is related to the Greek work *askein*, meaning "to train oneself." Ascetics leads us to think too quickly of abstinence. The primary meaning of the Greek noun *askēsis* is "exercise," or "training." It refers, thus, not to something negative (abstaining), but to something positive (exercise). We might recall Acts 24:16, where Paul says that he always exercises himself in order to have a clear conscience before God and men. He uses the word *askein* to describe that activity.

This positive meaning appears still more clearly when we consider another word that could be called a synonym of *askein*. To Timothy, Paul says, "Exercise yourself rather to godliness" (1 Tim. 4:7). The word translated "exercise" is *gumnazein*, familiar to us in the word *gymnastics*.

A well-known book about ascetics was written by Gisbertus Voetius, whom we mentioned earlier. In 1664 he wrote *Ta askētika sive exercitia pietatis* (Ascetics or exercises in piety). Voetius had written about these exercises especially for their use by the academic youth of his day.

He dealt with various subjects, like prayer, spiritual meditation, contrition, mourning, regular times of prayer (thrice daily), fasting and waking, vows, solitude, silence, temptations, and "spiritual abandonment." Attention was also devoted to reading and hearing God's Word, reflecting on the sermons one hears in church, and the meaning of the sacraments. The question of Sunday observance also occupied a place in his discussion. Even euthanasia appeared in the list of subjects, but in the ancient sense of the word: the art of dying in a Christian manner! A long chapter provides a thorough analysis of prayer. Here are some of the many questions Voetius answers: How often must one pray? Where? To whom? What should be our posture for prayer? What does "pray without ceasing" mean (1 Thess. 5:17)? How should one's prayer be organized? How and for whom should we give thanks? When may we use a quick prayer? What are the hindrances to prayer? The extent and earnestness of his discussion indicate how, for Voetius, all of life must be marked by prayer.

WHY DID IT FALL INTO DISUSE?

The theological subject of ascetics has fallen by the wayside. What occasioned that? I think that three factors have played a role.

In the first place, the practice of piety can be emphasized in such a way that people come to view ordinary daily living negatively. Very easily we get two kinds of people: those who are satisfied to do what is required, and those who perform a bit more than required. I am thinking here as well of the distinction between precepts (Latin: *praecepta*) and counsels (Latin: *consilia*) that appeared very early in the Christian church. (This distinction is related to the apostle Paul's comment in 1 Corinthians 7:25, which the Vulgate rendered *Praeceptum Domini non habeo, consilium autem do*: "I have no precept from the Lord, but I give a judgment.") The precepts supposedly indicate what each person's duty is, while the counsels are supposedly for people who are striving for a holier life. The holier life was for monks, for example, who obligated themselves by vows of poverty, obedience, and chastity. They turned away from the world in order to be more accessible to God than the ordinary person with his daily routines would be able to be.

In this way, the "spiritual" is easily exalted above the "natural." Clear examples of this are easy to find, even among Reformed thinkers. Here I would mention Theodore à Brakel (1608–69), who wrote a book about his own practices of piety. He registered this achievement with virtual silence about his wife and children, about the church and his office of minister, and about everything else happening in the world around him. We find nothing like this in Scripture, where we read about someone crying out in need, confessing his guilt, or offering his thanksgiving. These expressions usually involve enemies, family, or countrymen. In the prayers of the Bible, the world gets included.

It is not surprising that the kind of ascetics that developed in the direction of *mysticism* could never have been expected to flourish in the Reformed world. Mysticism turns the practice of piety into a spiritual acrobatics from which most people recoil—or about which they sigh that these grapes hang too high for picking. Ascetics of this kind generates an elite corps of initiates. But the practice of piety that Scripture describes must be something for every Christian.

In the second place, we see in ascetics a development that is similar to the one in casuistics. Everything is untangled and schematized. People construct a model for spiritual living that quickly becomes a prescription for everybody.

Little remains of Christian liberty, a freedom that needs space also with respect to forms of expression. What we have said about a casuistry that is too refined applies as well to this kind of ascetics.

But there remains one more reason for the demise of ascetics. We are dealing with a subject that is difficult for each of us. The Heidelberg Catechism says that prayer is the chief part of the gratitude we owe to God (Lord's Day 45). But we have a hard time setting aside fifteen minutes for it! Prayer requires inner peace and quiet. We are usually so busy with ourselves and others that it is a real chore to detach ourselves from our activities and set aside time for contact with God.

SPIRITUALITY: THE INDISPENSABLE CONTEXT

It would be regrettable if we lost the truly valuable benefits offered in the past in the area of ascetics, the twin of casuistics. However, it is no longer suitable to hang on to the term *ascetics*. The word has a negative ring that disappears when we speak, not of ascetics, but of *spirituality*. The spirituality I have in mind is the kind I described at the beginning of this chapter. Naturally, the word *spirituality* itself requires explanation. It can, in some people's use of the term, include everything. Every great religion includes spirituality and ascetics. It comes down to what we include in the term, and for Christians, reflecting on our fellowship with God, it includes the triune God as He has revealed Himself in Scripture.

Elsewhere I have written more extensively about what I think spirituality means in relation to ethics. I have written about this in connection with the Apostles' Creed, which summarizes briefly what it means to believe in the triune God (Douma 1993, chap. 2). Christian ethics cannot exist apart from this spiritual context. Christian ethics deals with interpersonal relationships. But *how* Christian ethics does this depends on the spirituality which determines its dynamic.

The great theologian Karl Barth (1886–1968) wrote a dogmatics (systematic theology) that he was unable to complete. For him, dogmatics and ethics were so related that he did not treat them separately; rather, in his *Church Dogmatics* he first treated the dogmatic aspect and then the ethical aspect. When he was ready to discuss concrete ethical issues, he began with perspectives on three issues: Sunday observance, confession as praise to God, and prayer. Approaching ethics this way is rather enchanting. We begin the week—and its many ethical issues—with Sunday. When we genuinely praise God and realize the power of prayer, the wrong paths of legalism or humanism are blocked at the trailhead.

Ethics is a serious endeavor that will avoid any spirit of oppressiveness and narrow-mindedness as long as it is nurtured by a good spirituality. Such spirituality must go beyond the theoretical to the concrete practice of piety, in prayer and in studying Scripture, on Sunday and at home. These are not frills, but absolute essentials for *responsible* conduct.

Literature

Douma, J. 1993. *Christelijke levensstijl.* 2d ed. Kampen: Kok.

Geesink, W. 1931. *Gereformeerde ethiek.* 2 vols. Kampen: Kok.

Kuyper, Abraham. 1909. *Encyclopedie der heilige godgeleerdheid.* 2d rev. ed. Vol. 3. Kampen: J. H. Kok.

Bibliography

GENERAL ETHICS

Frankena, W. K. 1973. *Ethics*. Englewood Cliffs, N.J.: Prentice-Hall.

Holmes, R. L. 1993. *Basic moral philosophy*. Belmont, Calif.: Wadsworth.

MacIntyre, Alasdair. 1967. *A short history of ethics: A history of moral philosophy from the Homeric age to the twentieth century*. London: Routledge and Kegan Paul.

MacIntyre, Alasdair. 1984. *After virtue: A study in moral theory*. 2d ed. Notre Dame: University of Notre Dame Press.

MacIntyre, Alasdair. 1990. *Three rival versions of moral enquiry: Encyclopedia, genealogy, and tradition*. Notre Dame: University of Notre Dame Press.

Mackie, J. L. 1990. *Ethics*. London: Cox and Wyman.

Singer, P., ed. 1991. *A companion to ethics*. Oxford: Blackwell.

CHRISTIAN ETHICS

Bloesch, Donald G. 1987. *Freedom for obedience: Evangelical ethics for contemporary times*. San Francisco: Harper & Row.

Brunner, E. 1937. *The divine imperative: A study in Christian ethics.* New York: MacMillan.

Davis, John Jefferson. 1985. *Evangelical ethics: Issues facing the church today.* Phillipsburg: P&R Publishing.

Douma, J. 1996. *The Ten Commandments: Manual for the Christian life.* Translated by Nelson D. Kloosterman. Phillipsburg, N.J.: P&R Publishing.

Henry, Carl F. H. 1979. *Christian personal ethics.* 2d ed. Grand Rapids: Baker.

Murray, John. 1984. *Principles of conduct.* Grand Rapids: Eerdmans.

O'Donovan, Oliver. 1994. *Resurrection and the moral order: An outline for evangelical ethics.* 2d ed. Grand Rapids: Eerdmans.

Thielicke, Helmut. 1979. *Theological ethics.* Edited by William H. Lazareth. 3 vols. Grand Rapids: Eerdmans.

White, R. E. O. 1981. *The changing continuity of Christian ethics.* Vol. 2, *The insights of history.* Exeter: Paternoster.

Index of Scripture

Index of Subjects and Names

J. Douma (Th.D., Theological College of the Reformed Churches in the Netherlands [liberated]) is respected internationally for his perceptive interpretation and careful application of Scripture in relation to contemporary ethical problems. He was professor of Christian ethics at the Theological University in Kampen from 1970 to his retirement in 1997. Among his publications is *The Ten Commandments: Manual for the Christian Life*.

Nelson D. Kloosterman (Th.D., Theological University in Kampen) is professor of ethics at Mid-America Reformed Seminary, where he has taught since 1984. He is also an author, translator, and seminar speaker on a wide range of issues.